# Praise for Unarmored

"Wise, poignant, and threaded with personal stories that feel universal, this book makes me feel reassuringly human and right on time. Allison Crow is a wise, non-guru-y guide into the underbelly of emotions. Read this book. Your inner parts will thank you."

— **DR. MANDY LEHTO, EXECUTIVE COACH AND HOST OF** **_ENOUGH, THE PODCAST_**

"Thank Gawd for putting Allison Crow on this planet. _Unarmored_ is for anyone who knows there's more to this life than getting better at getting by. Like all of the buck wild colors in her art, she has so many ways to reach us where it truly matters."

— **TRIPP LANIER, PROFESSIONAL COACH, AUTHOR OF** **_THIS BOOK WILL MAKE YOU DANGEROUS_**

"Allison Crow has created the most magnificent and significant book you will ever experience. _Unarmored_ is filled with truths, tenderness, and tenacity. She shares her stories, bares her soul, and invites you to welcome all of you and your parts into _being_."

— **DIANE BLECK, ARTIST**

"If you're looking for a book that will give you permission to be fully YOU, that will give you inspiration to do your work in the world, that will give you belly laughs so you can take life a little less seriously, look no further! Unarmored is a work of art and Allison Crow's fresh and wild take on life is just the thing the world needs right now."

— **AMY AHLERS, AUTHOR OF _REFORM YOUR INNER_** **_MEAN GIRL_**

"Great leaders don't need to learn any more about leadership. They've done all the learning. They've done all the reading. They need to UNLEARN. They need to strip away all the BS about how they 'should' show up.

This book is a must-read for leaders who want a roadmap to deep confidence. You'll laugh, you'll cry, and you'll become the risk-taking, courageous leader you've always wanted to be. No permission needed. Thank me later."

— RICH LITVIN, FOUNDER OF 4PC, AUTHOR OF
*THE PROSPEROUS COACH*

"Allison Crow unabashedly shares powerful personal stories about her life, stories that are raw and funny and full of so much earned wisdom. But she doesn't present these stories from the perspective of "here's what I learned, and I'm all better and enlightened now." She never portrays herself as someone who has all the answers . . . She is most interested in communicating about her messy, tender, confused, and tangled healing process and providing compassion for this healing process in herself and others. And that realness and commitment come across so beautifully in her new book, *Unarmored: Finding Home in the Wild Edges of Being Human*."

— CHRIS ZYDEL, WILD HEART QUEEN, FOUNDER
CREATIVE JUICES ARTS

"Allison Crow is one of those rare people who inspire us to grow by sharing her raw humanity, vulnerability, and deep wisdom. You will be changed forever, and for the better, by reading this book."

— MARK J. SILVERMAN, EXECUTIVE COACH AND
AUTHOR OF *ONLY 10S 2.0*

FINDING HOME IN THE
WILD EDGES OF BEING HUMAN

# Unarmored

♡ Allison Crow

**Compassionate Mind Collaborative**

*cmcollab.com*

This is a work of creative nonfiction. Some parts have been fictionalized in varying degrees, for various purposes.

Artwork by Allison Crow
Edited by Heather Doyle Fraser
Copyedited by Jo Linda Crow
Proofed by Julie Homon
Marketing by Jesse Sussman
Author Photo by Brooke Genn
Cover and interior layout by Cindy Curtis

*ISBN 978-1-7372006-9-7 (paperback)*
*ISBN 979-8-9869419-0-5 (ebook)*

First Edition: December 2022

This paperback edition first published in 2022

This creative work and expression from my unarmored heart is dedicated to my clients over the last twenty years, and to my Soul-friends who choose to live authentically, whole-heartedly, and humanly as ordinary extraordinary humans. Our reciprocal relationships inspire me to no end. Thank you for receiving my quirky, circular, and human leadership. I also dedicate this book to my quiet watchers — I feel you out there, holding me in love and appreciation, and it matters.

From my yellow heart to yours, this book is dedicated to you.

# Contents

## BY CHRIS ZYDEL

For over forty years, my professional and creative life has been spent exploring and expressing my creativity while also guiding my students to claim and honor their unique and individual creative being through expressive arts and intuitive painting.

I don't teach technique. And I don't help people to become better artists. I teach people to trust their intuition by engaging with the creative process. I teach people how to value their spirit-nourishing experience of simply being creative over any type of creative outcome. My work is not for everyone. It goes against the dominant cultural ideology, which gives people the message that creativity is only worthwhile if it brings you outer-world things like money, status, or approval. Many folks have a hard time letting go of those particular perks and are challenged to understand why being creative for its own sake is really what matters.

When Allison Crow participated (with great enthusiasm) in my Wild Heart Expressive Arts Teacher Training Program, I knew immediately that I was in the presence of a kindred spirit. From the very beginning, Allison got it. She already knew on a very profound level that honoring your creativity — or honoring your soul — is where true healing, wholeness, and authenticity live. I felt like Allison signed up for my program not so much to learn about this way of being creative but more to validate what she already knew deep in her bones. I could sense that she wanted to clear away the patriarchal conditioning she still carried with her. This conditioning only allows for pushing, striving, efforting, hustling, and being successful at all costs.

She came to be supported by her heart, body, and emotions instead of solely residing in her head. She came to release and heal the many layers of trauma we all carry from living in this culture through the sacred process of making art.

She came because she wanted a safe place and supportive community to help her become more and more unarmored as she revealed and reclaimed her truest self.

She came to express herself fully via the creative process without holding anything back.

And she did all of these things with much passion, gusto, and enthusiasm. When Allison decides she is doing a thing, she does it wholeheartedly. She brings all of who she is to whatever project she has decided to undertake.

This is why I was so excited to learn that she was writing a book about her journey as a coach, a businesswoman, and a gorgeously vulnerable human being.

What I love most about Allison is her commitment to being real. She doesn't pretend to be anything other than who she really is — which is so rare and refreshing — and is also totally committed to helping her many students and clients do the same. And that realness and commitment come across so beautifully in her new book, *Unarmored: Finding Home in the Wild Edges of Being Human.*

*Unarmored* is a book that is so necessary for the scary and tumultuous times we are experiencing right now. It provides a map for hope and inspiration as we tread into and through this new, radically changing world we are living in.

Allison unabashedly shares powerful personal stories about her life, stories that are raw and funny and full of so much earned wisdom. But she doesn't present these stories from the perspective of "here's what I learned and I'm all better and enlightened now." She never portrays herself as someone who has all the answers. Or any answers. She is most interested in communicating about her messy, tender, confused, and tangled healing process and providing compassion for herself and others. She is one smart cookie and has clearly devoted herself to her own personal growth and healing as well as the growth and healing of her many, many students and clients.

Allison offers insights and her own unique take on some potent and compelling tools that she has gathered over her years of self-exploration, like Internal Family Systems, developing nourishing habits, a sure-fire way to get out of your head and truly embody your emotions (once you read the chapter on fire ants, you won't ever see them, or the emotion of anger, the same way again). She also discusses nervous system regulation, Gabor Mate's work on authenticity and attachment, and much, much more. She explains some of these concepts using wildly colorful visual aids of her own art, which is the coolest thing ever. Allison is irreverent and hilarious and does not shy away from calling bullshit when she sees it. More than one sacred cow of the coaching and personal growth industry gets challenged and overturned on these pages. (Here's looking at YOU, Law of Attraction.)

One thing she consistently comes back to again and again and again is how true and lasting healing happens in our bodies and our feelings — NOT solely in our heads. And how only paying attention to shifting your mindset, or what she so brilliantly names the Positivity Bypass, keeps people stuck in unhelpful and unchanging patterns of behavior. And that what matters more than anything is being completely and unapologetically your true and essential self, which includes every last bit of who you are.

I could go on and on and on about everything Allison discusses on these pages. There is so much rich and juicy wisdom here. The thing that impressed me the most about this book, though, is that as much as it is chock full of wondrously helpful information — genius ideas about how to live and work and be, and potent personal teaching tales — it is at the core a powerful transmission of energy. Allison models how she lives and teaches in the way that she writes. I found myself impacted on a visceral nervous system level as the alchemy of her words and language entered into my body-being, bypassing my linear thinking brain, and allowing me to make deeply felt connections in ways that made no sense to my mind but opened hidden doorways into the deepest chambers of my heart. Be prepared for the ah-ha moments to come fast and furious as you dive into this kaleidoscopic world of her huge radiant spirit and dazzlingly incandescent mind.

This woman is a magician, a wizard weaving magic spells of permission and hope, compassion and presence, liberation and realness, trust and wholeness, reminding you on every page that who you are is always more than enough and all you ever need to be. She is a sacred cheerleader of the soul, a fierce mama bear of truth, and a courageous warrior of the spirit, guiding you, holding you, and tending to the sweetness of your vulnerable humanness with her huge, all-encompassing heart.

**— CHRIS ZYDEL, WILD HEART QUEEN, FOUNDER
CREATIVE JUICES ARTS**

# Unarmored

Nothing like picking up an inspirational personal development book and seeing someone's messes sprawled out on the pages up front, not just hidden in the middle-end-you-might-not-read-corners.

I'm not here to bullshit you, to make you believe in the pretty . . . but to believe in, and connect more deeply with, the HUMANness of this glorious life. Maybe this one lady, and this one crazy book, that is ultimately about leadership, will tell you more of the truth and give you a little permission to fall in love with your complex and human self.

Armor is heavy, I've carried protective gear forever, and it's all I've only ever seen in most of my mentors, even still. Underneath my armor is my humanness, my heart, my longings, my creativity, and the wholeness of all of my being.

Many days my armor and my desires compete. I can feel the tightness of my breastplate. My soul craves fullness and freedom. Parts of me want people, connection, collaboration, and community. However, my protectors often resist it fiercely, more concerned with safety. They fear me being rejected, ridiculed, unchosen, and unloved.

My armored protectors dread the idea of me feeling the pain of being unlovable and insignificant, and especially of "doing it wrong."

I witness this daily in my own being, and in glorious humans just like you. Once you recognize the signs of armor and protectors, the world looks different. Compassion grows. Our souls sense that recognition and compassion, and invite us deeper, wider, all the way to the edges — so that we might live Soul-FULL and whole.

Friends and colleagues sometimes tell me they are shocked at the things I share. OK. And what I know from tens of thousands of coaching conversations over eighteen years is that we all have a human side, just wanting to belong and be loved, but often it's hidden behind the armors we wear. And there, under that protective armor, we can never give nor receive the gifts we are here to share.

Piece by piece, I'm becoming unarmored, and I'm happy to share just a bit of that with you.

PART 1

# Cultivation

# Smarty ++

Who would I have to be, to write this book? What is the identity of the woman who has written and published this work? I have always seen myself as the woman who *wants* to write and publish inspirational memoirs and self-leadership books. I've found countless ways to kick the can of this dream down the road ahead of me. Until now, I have only been the woman who "wants to."

Who would I BE, what would my being, identity, beliefs, energy, and mindset BE if I was already the woman who had written the book? What would it require of my nervous system? How would I have led all the parts of me who resisted and threw protective, resistance-fits along the way?

This is *how* we will become the woman who has written the book. By learning to calm our nervous system and then by connecting with BEing. This is more than defying doubt with mindset. This is more than manifestation. This is Cultivation.

I wasn't born wanting to write books. I was born a pink-cone-headed six-pound baby who had no clue of what writing was or could be. I was born with no desire — except for the innate desire to be loved and cared for.

Then, all the things in the invisible systems of life told me what to desire and exactly how to desire it, and so I did.

I can't remember where I first learned of the "how to have it." Oh, wait, yes I can! I will tell you the story of my client Stacy P and her Gucci shoes later.

For now, I finally see, clear as day, the ability to have that which we want. I have it, and you can learn how to have it, too. And I'm rather aware of how this sounds so much like one of the old-white-men-written self-help books that declared, "everything you desire" is within reach if only you:

- Change your thinking to change your life.
- Find the feel-good place.
- Use the right manifesting language.
- Trade up your thoughts to the "most powerful" creation thoughts instead of these paltry scarcity and fearful thoughts.
- Change your being with your language.

Or whatever we have been promised. Am I about to become another *promiser*? Perhaps.

My Gawd! (That is what I shall call her, Gawd. She has a soft, southern drawl in my head.) My Gawd, I am totally thankful for those books and teachers and authors who promised me those things. They were mostly true, but not completely.

For forty-nine years, they provided direction and gave my brain a sense of hope. But my body never really discovered those words coming into real live form in my life. Until they did. That is precisely why I am finally able to write this book. If you are reading this book (thank you), I'm assuming you are what I will call a Smarty. Simply because you are *reading* a book. That is a big deal.

And, not only are you reading a book, you are reading this non-fiction book, which makes you a Smarty++ in my mind. Because you aren't just escaping into the magic of a story (I adore those, too), you are hungry for insights and ideas and creative flow and growth. You are a Smarty++.

We Smarty++, we love to learn. Learning, and growing, and reading, and studying is juicy and stimulating to us — at least until our brain is bored with one thing, until the next. We smarty here, and smarty there, and we get on the "keep learning new things train" because it is stimulating. Some accuse us of never sticking to one thing for very long. We collect books in three formats and pile them on our desks. We have a library of countless half taken online classes. We even watch TV and movies with Google, Wikipedia, and IMDB at our fingertips. As NBC once told us, *"the more you know the more you know."*

Marshall Goldsmith wrote a non-fiction book called *What Got You Here Won't Get You There*[1] and a few of my mentors used that title as a teaching phrase ad-nauseum. It would briefly cross my frontal lobe occasionally, and I would take note and give a mental, yeah, yeah, yeah.

Well, dang if Marshal Goldsmith wasn't correct! But reading his book wasn't what got me to the fullness of this wisdom. I tried to pick up the book (in the kindle version) and was annoyed to find a comic book inside — what a creative presentation — it was just toooooo much stimulation for my brain.

It was as if my new kindle reader was telling me, there is nothing I can learn in these books that means anything if I have not *lived* it in each and every cell of my body. Life provides the lessons so that *all* of me — body, heart, and mind — can learn.

And this is how my Smarty++ parts finally relented and relaxed, and gave way to a truly open heart, connected to my body, after hitting a dead end of *"what got you here won't get you there."* And, this is how my Smarty++ parts now live in a Calm, Connected, Compassionate, Curious, Clear, Creative, Confident, and Courageous state of being . . . most of the time.

For real, not all the time. But much of the time. And, I'm good with that.

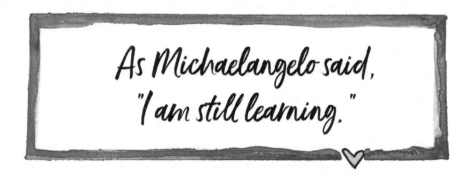

As Michaelangelo said,
"I am still learning."

I woke up in a second-floor room of a one hundred-year-old bunkhouse in Calistoga, California. The light was coming through the dated-country-floral curtains and I remembered that the election was yesterday, so I reached for my phone, assured that I would see the headlines "Hillary Clinton First Woman President."

But. I. Did. Not.

Like exactly half of the United States, I was gobsmacked and shocked. I had, after all, dismissed my husband's (and some political journalists') cynicism that what's-his-face could actually win. At the moment I rolled over and grabbed my phone off the nightstand, only to see *he* had won, my Smart Parts choked on their own intelligence and knowing, the way a machine gasps for air and completely quits working with a big, dark, puff of smoke.

I was in Calistoga on a nine-day painting retreat — one of four that year — with ten other women. We were painting to heal, painting to feel, and learning to teach others to do the same. And mercy, did we get the fucking opportunity to feel and heal.

That morning as we gathered in a circle, we were all aghast and horrified at the election results. But my friend Antoniette was visibly shaken to her core, almost catatonic. The rest of us had the systemic safety of our white skin and cis-genders, but Anto? Anto was black, and gay.

I was horrified in my mind, but Anto, who actually had been, at that time, diagnosed with terminal brain cancer, was terror-stricken in every cell in her body. She was more afraid of the ripple of this next presidential term than she was of her brain cancer.

After gathering in our circle, with heavy hearts, we were tasked to continue with the day's agenda, and so we did. Our first workshop of the day, led by a peer-facilitator, was quiet and somber. The heaviness of the shocking news was thick in the air. It was dense in my body, and the thickness was excruciating. Against our workshop guidelines, I broke the silence and cracked a sarcastic joke. Humor has, and still is, a way for me to disconnect from pain, and in that moment I involuntarily chose to disconnect.

The peer facilitator *shushed* me with a short, crisp, stinging word accompanied by a sharp glare, *"Shush."*

I bit the inside of my cheek to bleeding as my jaw clenched and my blood began to boil. She fucking *shushed* me! I finished the workshop in silence on the outside, but with searing rage on the inside.

After the workshop finished and as we rounded the circle, each giving our constructive feedback, I got hotter and hotter inside. When it was my turn to give constructive criticism, long gone was any adult version of me. At first, a controlled and nervous part of me tried to deliver helpful, polite language for how a teacher could, without the shame of a *shush*, redirect a student who was breaking the silence rules. After all, I have a master's degree in adult education, and have thirty years of facilitation and teaching experience.

Just as this meek, yet trained, educated, determined part of me began to speak, an angry, volatile teenage part from deep inside pushed right past and unloaded on the facilitator.

"Who the FUCK do you think you are? Shushing me like a FUCKING dog," I screamed as I stood up and leaned forward to make myself appear bigger.

As soon as I realized I'd lost my shit on her, in front of my peers, and my beloved teacher, another part of me stepped in. A part of me I call "Shrinking Shame" flooded my body and thoughts, "I'm leaving, I'm getting in my car and going to the airport *now*." I trembled, trying to pretend I was strong.

As I began to bolt from the group, the bulky arrangement of the couches arranged into a clunky circle, the warm voice of my mentor stopped me. "You can leave if you want to, but I hope you will stay." Her voice was calm, not shocked at all, and just soothing enough to give me space to leave without actually leaving all the way.

One woman gave my body something no book could ever give me. In a moment of threat, she let my body and my nervous system know it was safe to BE, even raging, with her. Although still shaking, I stayed. For the first time, with the help of a beloved wise woman, so full of SELF energy, I didn't leave. I didn't leave the retreat, I didn't leave myself.

Up in my room, later that night, having apologized and reconciled with the victim of my vitriol, I was left with the horrified voices of my parts, "Scolding Shame" and "Confusion" screaming through my thoughts, "I know better. How can I lose control like that? How can a part of me be so wise, and then, another part completely loses my shit when it comes to practicing the wisdom I teach every damn day."

It was moments like those that helped me see, no matter how much coaching and learning I did, I still wasn't free. No matter how many books I read, I never achieved those promises. Over the years these moments would creep up on me, often in explosions — I would be fine one moment and flooded the next, with what seemed to be younger, terrified versions of me — my brain and intelligence of being in my forties and being overtaken by a three, or seven-year-old version of me, in all her desperation.

I've been certified since 2012 in a modality that does inner parenting work. I've done inner child work and healing over the years, and experiences like these let me know there were more parts of me to be unearthed, more of me to meet.

The work in my head was just the front porch of my becoming all of me.

# Hello Heart and Soul

I see you.
I am here for you.
I will not leave you.
I am listening.

Come inside.
Come be with me.
Here you will find the calm you seek.
Put all of the other sources down
and
Source inside.

I came into this world hearing the messages of my heart and soul. Fully intertwined with Spirit, I could *hear* what my heart was saying . . . until I couldn't. The world got noisy, as it does for all of us. I don't remember when or how it happened. It was subtle . . . that slow, smothering of Self in service of the rules, the opinions of others, and the ways of ordinary life.

What was once confidently clear and open became confusing, constricted, and conflicted. But my heart and soul never left me. No matter what walls I constructed, or how I kept her fiercely guarded, she continually and gently whispered, and on occasion, ached in my body for attention.

For years, instead of listening to my soul, heart, or body, I let my head take the lead. Years of heartbreaking moments and relationships made it convenient to escape into my brain, my intellect, my "mindset," and my cognitive capacity.

And still, my soul, heart, and body waited patiently.

They knew. They trusted me to get lost. They knew that getting lost would be the path to genuinely coming home to myself. They knew that learning to *trust myself* would cause me to completely and wholly *meet myself*, so that I could fully *be myself* with an open and unburdened heart.

# Unchosen

At twenty-seven and a single woman in graduate school, I bought my first home out in the hill country of Texas. As I was changing the laundry one day, from the other room I heard the sound of, "You've got mail" from my 100mb IBM computer (yes, just like the movie). And there he was, in my online inbox — the one I had been waiting for — my nice, sweet, and professional man. We had a giddy falling in love, full of romantic gestures, meeting the parents, and even a new puppy together. He fit the fairytales, and I was expecting a happily ever after.

Two years later we were married in the big expensive wedding I'd always dreamed of, in front of two hundred friends and family members. When I put on my wedding dress, I broke out in hives. Perhaps I should have paid attention. My body was pleading with me. I'd never before and never since had an allergic reaction to clothing. Looking back at the photos, I now see the terror in his face and the hives on my neck instead of the calm yet passionate adoration every couple imagines they will feel on the Big Day.

Two years and one move-up-home after getting married, I arrived home from teaching school and he was there, at 4:00 p.m., waiting for me. This was unusual. My gut sank. Something was wrong.

He had come home early to tell me he was leaving and didn't want to be married anymore.

I genuinely loved and adored him, and after he walked out, I slid down the white wooden door until my body came to rest in a sad and broken slump on the hardwood floor. The ache in my heart wasn't just in my mind. The tears I'd held back during his soft and meek "I'm leaving" speech released in sobs as if I'd never, ever, cried before. I couldn't breathe, or move, or think. I sat there for hours in the dark. My heart literally hurt — a thick, tight, aching filled my chest. My dreams and my ambition were broken. And my deepest fear had just come true. I was unchosen and left.

What was wrong with me? If there was no other woman, if there was no scandal or drug problem, and my sweet, nice-guy husband wanted a divorce, then I was just being unchosen for being me. Again. That was the biggest ache of all. I didn't understand what I had done to be left. Surely my "goodness" as a wife, or in the world, hadn't deserved this pain.

I never expected perfection in marriage, but I had held it in my personal construct that marriage was something to fight for. In the three therapy sessions I insisted upon, there was no movement or desire from him. I wanted to work it out, fix what was wrong, hear how I could be better and stay together. Nothing I could say or do would move his compass. Even my therapist acknowledged that he was already long gone. He'd made up his mind months before he walked out the door. All that was left was the formal untying of legal knots and the papers from the court saying our marriage was legally over.

This was the abrupt end of my marriage and my young lady dreams. When I tried to look forward, I only felt left . . . left by him, left also by a few Christian friends who dared not stay close with me for fear of tainting themselves. They saw my divorce as sin and an unforgivable abomination. They left and unchose me as if divorce was a contagious disease.

I saw my husband moving out of our life together, and that leaving brought with it all the fears I'd had since childhood. I felt that pleading coming up from my gut as my husband put down the ties of our marriage. It's the same feeling I had every time I saw my Dad walk out the door when he and Mom fought when I was growing up. At that moment, I was a child again — heart broken, sad and scared, and sure he would never come back. "Pleeeeeease don't leeeeeave," careened the broken cry throughout my body and my being. I felt the tornado come in and decimate the pleasing path I thought I'd found for my life.

In reality, this wasn't a decimation of anything. It was the beginning of my very own self-creation. It shattered the bullshit story I told myself about how life was going to be. It disintegrated contrived plans plucked from a little girl's naive heart. That heartbreak left me in the mess of my *real* life. It was the beginning of discovering my authentic self, and it set me on a course I never knew I would enjoy so much.

When my husband left, something primal clicked in me. I went into survival mode for myself. Our house had been purchased on mostly his salary and I was determined to keep the central Austin home I loved. That meant changing course job-wise, and making some serious bank. Thirty-six thousand as a private school teacher was not going to cut it. There was no option for me to not succeed. It was my first big bet on myself. This was the hard right turn and unanswered prayer that opened my life to gifts I might never have given myself. Just-fine desire was replaced with an immediate driven need to pay my mortgage on my own, and to rise up. I became a REALTOR®.

While I am prone to hyperbole and exaggeration, I cannot see any other way I would have decided to go into business for myself. A new job, maybe, but never self-employment, sales, or a small business. I never considered that I might actually have joyful, satisfying ambition in the direction of work. It took years for me to see the strength and love my ex had to walk away. He knew before I did. He didn't even know what he knew, he just knew. He had the courage to leave.

Being unchosen broke my heart. It broke all my plans. It was my ultimate fear. I thought I had done and been all the right things — be the nice girl, and find and fall in love with the "nice guy" and you will be safe. Then my "nice guy" left. It stripped my life of preprogrammed plans and order and set me wandering in a new kind of wilderness. Except, my being stripped of all the expectations gave me a fuel I'd not experienced before. For the first time in my life, I had to consider that I might not get married and have kids. I might have to do this thing — life — on my own. And if I did have to do it — I was going to do it — then fucking, happy, professional success was the only option.

I was in it for the glorious, highly esteemed I-told-you-so-revenge success, not just barely-get-by-pay-the-bills success.

That wilderness became the path that led me to discover and embrace the authentic part of me that was there all along, waiting underneath everything else. When everything I thought I knew fell apart, all that was left was for me to begin creating and experimenting — to begin cultivating. As my original ambitions of being a wife and mother disintegrated, I surrendered to the process that most of the stories omit.

Most stories tell of the fall and then glorify the happy ending and leave out the middle. You know what's in the middle? The process. The process doesn't always make good Hollywood. But the process is where the juice of life really lives. Artists thrive in the process. Souls KNOW the process is the gold that lasts, unlike the short-term dopamine hit of a flashy one-time result whose glimmer fades in quick time.

Process, inner work, trauma healing, the building of self trust, and personal growth don't always look sexy. I have found the sacred and holy of life are in the process, in the unfolding and exploration; they live in the middle, not the end. Process is messy, crazy, delicious, hilarious, sad, exhausting, colorful, expansive, excruciating, wonderful, and is never done! Some days I hate it, and on other days I am utterly high in the flow and holy gift that is the process.

Leaving behind the spell of our conditioning and embracing the process is where the real magic lives.

# Art Is Life

Once upon a time, I taught at a small Catholic school. In my first class of 28 students, there was a boy called Ramón[2]. Ramón was smart and curious. He excelled at math and reading, and when we would use crayons, he always and only used cerulean blue. It was his favorite color.

One day, while observing the students during free draw time, I saw that Ramón had drawn a landscape scene. Grass — cerulean blue. Trees — cerulean blue. A little boy — cerulean blue. Sunshine — cerulean blue. My co-teacher was observing, too. She was way more experienced than I, the obvious lead in the room, and I dare say she got this one wrong. All wrong.

When she saw Ramón's drawing, she got down to eye level with him and told him very clearly, "Sunshines are not blue. Why don't you try yellow or orange?" she asked, not from curiosity but with expectation.

I saw Ramón's face flush pale with shame and his head drop in disappointment. I tried to chime in and say, "I don't know Mrs. C., I've seen a blue sunshine or two, and art can be any color," but it was too late. Ramón was crushed. While he was confident in academics, he was still exploring his creativity and a trusted adult told him he was wrong. This wasn't math. At the tender age of five little hearts bend to be loved and accepted.

No classmate or child ever questioned Ramón's cerulean blue. I never saw Ramón use that crayon color again. His whole world was that color until someone important told him what color his world *should* be.

Because I was also the computer instructor and technology coordinator at that school, I had the opportunity to teach every child in our K-8 school, not just kindergartners. Remembering how much every single one of my kindergarten students obsessively loved to draw, I decided to take a poll among all my students. I asked each grade the same question: "Are you an artist?"

Every single kindergartener said yes, joyfully and enthusiastically. Almost every second grader said yes. By third grade, only half of the girls still said yes. By fifth grade, only boys were willing to claim their artist selves, and only about a third of them. By eighth grade, only two in the entire grade were willing to say they were artists — both were boys.

Obviously, this wasn't a true research study, just my little small sample poll. It was, however, very telling about how authentic expression and identity can be smothered out in the systems of school and society.

What color is *your* world? Do you remember? Or has the world told you how it should be? I dare you to remember. Remember your colors. Remember that you are an artist. If you can't remember, choose to make your life a work of art. Choose whatever you want. Make the art of life that pleases you.

We are given a life full of moments that are all opportunities for choice, and for much of our lives, many of us are just moving through these moments without awareness, consideration, and the knowledge that we can cultivate our lives in so many ways. Like Pavlov's dogs, people-pleasing is trained into many of us.

They say I should . . . and so I do.

They won't love me if I don't . . . so I don't.

What will they think . . . and so I bend.

I should be this way or that way . . . and so I twist and
turn the true me into something I don't recognize.

The strong reward bell of approval rings each time we fall in line.

We are taught that "other" is more important than self, and so
we respond in a way that rings that bell, instead of cultivating an
authentic life and way of being in the world.

We are all conditioned. We bend and mold these precious parts
of ourselves to meet core needs, such as belonging, acceptance,
certainty, and even survival. We self-smother out of the deep, quiet
fear that we will be UN-connected and UN-loved. It just *is*.

An age-old question is nature or nurture. Scientists have debated
this for ages, and there is simply a complex entanglement of the two,
plus one missing ingredient. That ingredient is YOU. And me. Our
lived experiences plus the choices and decisions we make in the act
of intentional cultivation.

As a kid, painting and making art was play. Or was it? Was the
process really life all along and it just got adulted out of us? I don't
remember exactly when the play went out of art and life, and I'm not
sure if Ramón does either. I just know it went away until I decided to
bring it back, on purpose.

Painting (or making art, or music, or writing) is cultivation, it is
creation, it is exploration and experimentation, and play. I forgot all
this until in my mid-thirties when I was leading business trainings
with an array of rainbow-colored whiteboard markers (instead of the
lame black-blue-green-red four-pack that comes standard in most
training rooms).

My boredom in a real estate training room gave me the need to
bring fresh color to the whiteboard, and this led me down a creative
path, that, in the span of three short years, unfolded like this:

➡️ Bored with the four-pack of colors led me to

➡️ Rainbow-colored dry erase markers led me to

➡️ Formal training and education in Visual Thinking and Graphic Facilitation which led me to

➡️ An urge to leave the strict containers of corporate facilitation, even with color which led to

➡️ Wild, free, intuitive, messy, thick, juicy, colorful, untrained painting on canvas. Really BIG canvas.

Looking at a blank canvas is so different from a corporate fill-in-the-blank training or paint-by-numbers structure. One has to weed through all of the "shoulds" and "supposed to" rules floating around in our brains. One has to willingly put down all the externally conditioned pressure and any idea of the right way to even begin. The freedom of a blank canvas can be anxiety-inducing and full of the muscle memory of dread.

> To make a mark on a blank canvas, to write a word on a blank page... these are courageous acts of cultivation and self-trust. To take that first step is a reclamation of your own authority and sovereignty.

One must mentally, emotionally, and physically set aside all the stories from outside our heads and histories, into the present moment of possibility. No amount of wishing, daydreaming, taking another course, coaching, therapy, watching others, meditating, or manifesting will make that mark for you. Comparison or copying will not serve us here, those will only shrink your capacity to make your own authentic marks.

Make the mark.

Just the first mark. There is absofuckinglutely no wrong way to make a mark, so go for it. From your being and body onto the page, make the mark.

After the first mark we can breathe because we started. It's gone from an idea to energy in motion. Energy begets energy, and eventually that invites flow. Flow will never just smack you or me in the head from a stationary position. We must dare to move, even if gently, in the direction of the flow we want to create. At the canvas, with all the colors smeared out on a palette, and a stack full of brushes and mark-making tools — there is only opportunity to make more marks, one after the other in a grand experiment.

In painting on canvas — like life, it is not two dimensional. There are layers, and textures, and the possibilities are endless until you decide, from within your being and in communication with the spirit of your creation, that your painting is complete. There are no mistakes, and like life, every mess leads to a more magnificent collection of marks. Each of the marks reveal something. Each mark teaches you a piece of the great mystery without giving you the whole picture.

Often, when you have an idea of what a painting *should* look like, what the final outcome will be, that painting will laugh in your face until you take the stick out of your ass, relax a little and get back to a bit of mysterious and delirious surrender. That, of course, is easier said than done, and in every painting there is an "I-hate-you-this-sucks-ass-fuck-this-I-quit-and-want-to-burn-it-to-ashes" phase.

In this phase of creation, the skill is to meet these parts with compassion, connection, presence, and curiosity, not to shove them away or see it as failure. This is the *magic* of the fucking creation and it never goes away. Unless you put it away. Unless you throw away your cerulean blue crayon and suppress your urge to create a cerulean sun. Every road block in the process leads us to the gold in the outcome — yet we resist it, suppress it, judge it, and condemn ourselves for it. Stop doing that.

With presence, connection, and listening within, eventually each mark — fueled by your own energy — gathers together in a collection of marks to make a complete painting. And then you know what most artists do, because they can't not? Artists who create paintings, like artists who create life, grab another blank canvas and start making more glorious fucking marks because being free to create without the rules and systems, and the pressure to perform is the liberation no one else can give us. Nature didn't give it to you. Nurture probably didn't happen for you as a child, so you must — of your own accord — be brave enough to choose it.

# You are a Gardener, Not a Machine

Consistency. Production. Accomplishment. Success. Performance. Perfection. Growth. Expansion. Enlightenment. Arriving.

Despite what the invisible systems in society might expect from you — what mass messaging might tell you — you are a gardener, not a machine. Our culture and society prizes performance and productivity — we are pushed and pulled to create outcomes while ignoring process. What if we acknowledged and celebrated the process though? What if we remembered our humanness, our cycles, our becoming? What if?

When you are driven to perform, it's an impossible standard to maintain and sustain. I'm not an absolutist here, there is value in taking action, implementation, creating goals, etc. But it's not the whole picture, is it?

I started out my coaching career as a performance and productivity coach. I remember a time when I was on a coaching call back in the performance days. It was my job to report numbers, numbers, numbers, numbers, numbers. What does the data say? Did the numbers point to production? Were my clients producing enough? Was I producing enough? How many calls? How many leads? How much money did our clients create for the company?

Numbers without context — numbers alone — didn't give the complete picture of what was happening.

532.

What does that mean? You don't know. I don't know. Without context it's just a neutral meaningless set of numbers. Five hundred and thirty-two dollars? Great. Five hundre[...]two snakes under your house. Not so great. Numb[...] can be valuable for assessing information [...] that involves human beings, who are [...]

Inevitably, on any given call, [...] somebody's numbers were do[...] asked, "Wouldn't it be helpful to [...]ation from our clients? Like, is there a [...]eir world that might affect the numbers?["...]t's numbers were really far down, but her husband had died [...] after that, she had been diagnosed with cancer. The picture becomes a little clearer with these facts in mind. Context matters when we consider humanness. Machines are expected to perform with precision, consistency, and perfection.

We don't have to be a victim of our circumstances, but sometimes the circumstance, the context, and the landscape of what's going on absolutely, and most naturally, affect our performance. It makes sense that what we experience in life will impact our business because we are gardeners, not machines. We are human.

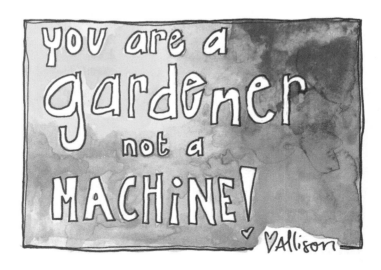

Performance isn't the only value in being human. Yet, many of us are conditioned to this way of thinking. If we aren't *doing*, are we even valuable? Performance will trick you into thinking that doing is the only path to value. I call bullshit. Productivity might be one section of your garden, but it is not your value or your worth.

Productivity — especially the American version — is killing us. We've been taught that more is better, and that productivity, at all costs, is "good." The almighty dollar is our idol. It's rewarded in our society, but at what cost?

Since you are here reading this book, I'm going to assume you are probably someone who really want___ __ well and BE well in the world, and you also want to keep _____ __. We don't want to just live and work. We want to _____ joy, deep and soul-full satisfaction, with lovin_____munities, and with regard for our plan___

Your soul in your huma_____ trying to make it regimented, consistent _____-blocked, productive, and accomplished. _____ mentally and systematically sold an imp_____

When you forget that you _____ machine, you end up buying shit you don_____ways to cope in the world that further empties your soul in an effort to satiate those subtle, little cravings. When we are hungry, angry, lonely, tired, and our souls are empty, we can be controlled and manipulated, we can be lulled into unconsciousness. We stay at war with and at the whim of the invisible, and not always benevolent, systems. We lose connection and presence with our own true selves.

Ask yourself, "Who benefits when I force myself to become a machine and produce at all costs?" It probably isn't you and your beloveds. It certainly isn't your sacred soul.

When we remember that we are gardeners, organic and natural beings, and that we can cultivate and create in the direction of our instincts and desires, we can step into conscious intention by calibrating our productivity, our rest, our spirituality, our health, and the

*[handwritten note: The problem is not everyone is motivated in self growth so you need to have productivity.]*

wellsprings of our joy. We can meet the difficulties we face not just with plans, but with self-connected and intuitive care.

If we think about our humanness as a garden, your dream garden is likely different from mine. We probably live in different climates, and you have plants you'd like to grow that are different from the ones that please me. We could each close our eyes and imagine two entirely different, yet both exquisite gardens, that is just the vision. What about the plan and the path to cultivating and caring for these gardens?

There are so many different phases and elements in cultivating a garden. We need to create space and time for planting seeds, we need to nurture and till the soil. We need to have patience for the growth and wait, tending the garden regularly, watering the plants and flowers and pruning the weeds. We don't need to water the weeds. When I tend to the garden in my own backyard, it doesn't necessarily require the same thing every single day, or even every week. We must consider the weather and the elements, and we may shift the course of our plans and care as new considerations arise. Above all, our garden, and our way of BEING a cultivator of that garden, are divinely unique.

You are a one-of-a-kind, uniquely-you, gardener, dear human, not a machine.

This little metaphor can work for so many areas of your life — including your business. It has been said that necessity is the mother of invention, so instead of creating a just-like-it's-always-been-done business, what if you regularly connected with the energy and entity of your business and considered questions like this:

- Internal climate check-in: What is the state of my nervous system? Am I regulated and calm, or am I inflamed, hijacked, or in any form of reaction? Is there any centering or soothing I need?

- What does my business need today? And is that need from a centered place, or are there parts of my business that are dehydrated and need specialized attention?
- What do my body, my mind, my heart, and my creative spirit need today?
- Is my current inner and outer tempo conducive to what I'm cultivating?
- What is the current landscape in the world around me?
  - In the market where I serve?
  - In the people with whom I work?
  - In the communities where I live?
- Is there any specific context to note if I zoom way in? What if I zoom way out and look at a long term view, and then an even longer term view?
- I will adjust each moment and the plan — even the longer term plan — according to all of the elements.
- Am I remembering or forgetting my true nature and essence as I move forward in my business this week, and what would support me in being aligned and rememBEring?

Just like planning and caring for a garden, cultivation requires deliberate consideration over rote automation. We've had some tumultuous weather recently — literal climate change weather patterns and massive cultural change. Our gardens might be a little parched, might have some hail damage, or maybe some of our roots are rotting. In times of uncertainty, disruption, and stress, the things that worked before might not work in the same way in this new environment. And we, as gardeners, are different beings, too! During these monumental and significant disruptions, I want to remind you — very lovingly — that you are not alone, even if things seem weird. Wobbly is a part of the process.

While we're here, let's address the wobble.

Feeling wobbly, full of doubt? These are not problems; there is nothing wrong with you. Wobble, doubt, anxiety, fear, and all their fellow uncomfortable parts are signals — they show up as an element of the growing process. Your mind and your body are trying to get your attention, so that you can re-center and drop into care and consideration from a slow, calm, and present place.

Sometimes the perfect time to slow down and take a look at the landscape is when things feel and seem weird. Wobbly. Your mind may be telling you to do all your normal "things," but your body and your environment might be giving you a different message. If your garden is already saturated, you need to take a break from watering it. Rest and integration are just as important to the lifecycle of a garden as planting and pruning.

So often we accidentally move around the world led by the parts of us that are fearful and afraid. The coping mechanisms and inner managers are desperate for exact certainty and a plan. These parts of us can be grasping, dehydrated, striving — and action taken from this place falls flat and can trigger a whole new cluster of parts — shame, resentment, and even more frantic fear.

Cultivation doesn't just scrape away all the squirming and protective parts of us with a giant bulldozer. (Even these squirming and protective parts are well-meaning; they are just not in their right aligned roles. They need our leadership and compassion.) Cultivation meets those parts, giving them presence and curiosity. This meeting allows the parts to relax so that we can drop into a deeper self-connection and awareness, and then practice consideration sourced from Creativity.

It does not do my garden any good to go out and water and fertilize excessively if that's not what my garden needs. I have a fiddle leaf fig. She is so finicky. If I water her too much, she starts to rot and die. Of course I'm not saying neglect your life or business. I am saying meet and manage the moment with consideration and care. Disconnect from groupthink for a while, from what everybody else is doing in their garden, pull away from the technology. Take some space to be present and connect with yourself. Slow, mindful, presence with yourself brings clarity. And it requires self-connection.

How do we connect with ourselves?

There are numerous ways to do this, and any self-proclaimed self-help guru will give you their version of what connecting with yourself looks like. But when I talk about managing the moment, I am also talking about taking stock of exactly what you are experiencing. What is in your mind? What sensations are in your body? Can you sense your deepest knowing? What do you notice about others around you and what they might be experiencing under the surface?

When I am feeling heavy, depressed, overwhelmed, or uncertain, one of the first things I do is slow way down and really check-in with myself. Getting back to center resets everything. Slow, from the inside out, one cell at a time, one breath at a time. Creating space for our poor overstimulated nervous systems to soothe and rest. Because there is so much around me that is NOT Self-connection, it takes a little time, especially if I'm really wonky or wobbly, to fully reconnect with me.

These days, I can feel my body saying "less computer, more music and dancing." Normally music and dancing are not one of my go-to's but, when I slow down and listen, I can feel my body craving it. Often, after hours at my desk in front of the computer, that's what my garden is asking for. If you ever feel like things are weird, and you are yearning for something you haven't yearned for before, you're not alone.

What if we allowed the feelings and the yearnings just as we allow our gardens to need different things at different times? What if we gave ourselves what we needed and met our soulful cravings with care? This is what human SELF-leadership looks like. What if the funk and the weirdness is *not* something to be ignored? Or bypassed? Or disciplined through? And certainly not shoved the fuck down into the hidden spaces in our bodies (behind layers of armor).

What if we met ourselves with compassion and consideration and curiosity?

What if we listened within more often?

What does my body need right now?

What does my mind need right now?

What does the sweet spirit of my business want from me?

I am listening.

I am here for all of me.

Most of us are trained to be fucking machines in business and in life. We are not trained to ask ourselves these questions. I'm over it. Nature doesn't hurry and it still blooms. There is a time for death and destruction, there is a time for rest. There is a time for going within. Maybe this is your time for going in. Maybe the current landscape or the current climate is requiring more of you just for everyday life. Right now, you may not have as many emotional or energetic resources, and yet, you're comparing your energy reserves to last year or last spring, or even worse, when we were twenty-six. Every season is different and every garden is different. When we fall into the temptation of comparing, despair grows and our blooming shrivels.

Here's what gardening in your small business might look like: Trust yourself to know what you need. Trust yourself to try different things. When you're in the beginning phases of business you have to noodle through experiment after experiment. Use your brain. Use your breath. Use your intuition and creativity. Make shit up! Noodling through is doing the best you can with the resources you have, taking some action and putting forth some effort. On the flip side — and this is part of trusting yourself — you need to rest and take care of yourself. Rest and nurturing practices are often kept as the reward for "hard work," but what if they are the *catalysts* for optimal creativity and clarity?

Visioning and dreaming can be energizing and motivating. Creativity and clarity can also set off fears and parts of us that want to stay safe. Running a small business is already a heavy load, and it can instinctually trigger shameful and heavy mind chatter, creating an invisible weight. Mental load and the burden of continual thinking stress is physically heavy in your body and can kill your dreams. Thoughts of "I'm doing it wrong," and "what's wrong with me that it's taking so long to succeed," are thick and capacity draining, but because they are invisible we often miss the physical and energetic impact they have on us. Learning to compassionately care for the parts of you that bring the mental fears and protective strategies will *support* your overall capacity and energy.

Balance isn't impossible. It's not mythical either. You have to cultivate a balance of work and life. Your brain wants to tell you it is half work, half rest, and half play. See what I did there? Three halves don't make a whole. You already know it is not fifty/fifty, or even thirds. Balance isn't static. It's mysterious, ever-changing, and often a gentle combination of balance and counterbalance — moment by moment, usually asymmetrical. Balance is the ultimate game of whack-a-mole.

As someone who adores, and feels deeply fulfilled by her work, it is difficult for me to admit this. It doesn't actually cultivate the life and garden I desire to be, all enthralled and focused on our businesses (as is often the case for the self-employed and entrepreneurial). I recognize a similar juxta-position when the Texas weather is so fresh, so gorgeous, in March, but then becomes hot, steamy, thick, and still in August. I, too, have cycles of growth and bloom, and then I have seasons of basking in the still, hot contentment of my creations, with little energy for effort. Parts of me often become distressed when I'm striving; other parts seem distressed when I am resting.

The drive and responsibility can suck me in, drag me down, and eventually grind me down and wear me out. How about you? It's taken twenty-five years, but I finally *know* I need a little bit of joy and a ton more of remembering the small moments and tiny accomplishments to nourish my creative heart. I need to spend time and become aware of the things I'm grateful for and the things I do that foster my SELF-trust and inner calm.

When you do this — when you remember and feel gratitude — you aren't bypassing the difficult things going on in your world. We are acknowledging the little moments of goodness that occur alongside the weirdness or the difficult. We are gardeners not machines. We are people of range. We can be willing to feel discomfort and simultaneously be willing to celebrate both micro and macro moments of success and joy.

But what if you do consider yourself more of a machine? What then? If you consider yourself to be more of a machine when it comes to business, I want you to be like the bottling machine at the Spoetzl Brewery in Shiner, Texas. The Shiner Beer company allows visitors to visit the brewery and see where and how all their beer is made. When you go on the tour, you can see the big vats for brewing the beer. Up on the second floor, there's a huge window, where you can look down and view the bottling manufacturing process. They brew, bottle, package, and then load the beer on delivery trucks. On these tours you can see the whole process, from beginning to end.

Seeing the entire process of the beer being made and then packaged was like watching a clip from the opening of *Laverne & Shirley* (an American sitcom on ABC from 1976 to 1983 that I watched during my childhood). After being brewed in big copper vats, the beer goes into the bottles, then caps are put on the bottles, and the bottles receive labels — all on an automated machine. When the bottles have just had the labels applied, they've been capped and they're full of beer, they go through a final step: all the bottles come around a curve in the production line in a single file line. At the moment they come around the corner, occasionally the centrifugal force causes a bottle to *wobble*! And when one of the bottles wobbles, the whole machine senses the wobble, and the entire production line slows down. The slowing down stops the centrifugal force and the bottle rights itself, or, if required, a human being overseeing the production line comes and corrects the bottle that tipped over. Once upright, the machine senses the bottle is back on track and it gets going again at a faster pace.

This machine has a mechanism built to adjust for the wobble.

If you don't like the gardener analogy, and you prefer to be a machine, please be a machine that accommodates for the wobble. When you are in the wobble, remember that it is part of the process, and also remember that you can slow down and trust yourself. You have the tools to navigate the wobble:

Breathe in.

Breathe out.

Focus on your work instead of the work of others.

Nurture your insides.

You know what's coming: small bites, incremental steps, asking for what you want and need.

Create every day.

Walk every day.

Dare to be rich, not just in money, but in Spirit.

No matter where you are, or what has happened, the flow always comes back and seasons return.

You are a gardener, not a machine. And if for some reason you want to be a machine, be a machine that accommodates the wobble with care.

# Inspired Action and Habits

For years I was really stubborn about inspired action *versus* habits. The thought of habits and discipline made me cringe. To me, inspired action equaled fun and ease; habits equaled boring and hard.

There was a time in my life and business when I was very influenced by *the law of attraction*. I was also very influenced (and still am) by the *law of action and embodiment*. The law of attraction, at that time, was such a soft and beautiful balm for me when I came out of the severe world of corporate sales in real estate. Maybe you know that world . . . making one hundred sales calls in a day, meeting obscene quotas, or having fifteen coaching sessions a day. Productivity + Success = Money, and that's all that matters.

After years of pushing, the promises of ease and manifesting with the law of attraction felt really good. It felt like a place to rest my burned-out soul. After excelling in a very constrictive corporate world, I let myself sink into the buttery balm of dream, and vision, and focus, and "hold your thinking at a high vibration, and all your dreams will manifest."

Once I landed there, I wanted to stay there. For many, many years, I only favored inspired action. And when I favored inspired action, it worked every single time, I ain't gonna lie. However, what it also did was leave gaping holes in my business, in my energy, and in my profitability and sustainability.

During this season, I was doing a giant amount of *doing*. Creation and action are often easy for me. I was prolific in my creation for life, in my coaching practice, and in creating art, content, offerings, retreats, and on and on and on.

This was a bright and delicious season in my business. Colorful, creative, expressive, mostly joyful, and full. But in my mid-forties when my body started to change, it couldn't keep up with the pace of my inspired action. Also, I wasn't often "inspired" to save for taxes and allocate my income in ways that were supportive, smart, and sustainable. Inspired actions served my craving for dopamine hits and social media engagement, but ultimately, they compromised my health and my financial peace.

Inspired action is for those of us that move fast, with lots of ideas. And many small business owners and entrepreneurs favor inspired action because we are willing to take risks and go fast. You can't be in this self-employed world without a little of that willingness. So for those of us who take risks and go fast, inspired action is stimulating and challenging and requires us to move which can be satisfying. And when we work like this, we often see results quickly. Dang! That satisfaction and thrill feel good!

Eventually, though, as we practice this inspired action over and over, we may have difficulty doing anything else. If we're fueled with inspired action only, what happens in real life if you go through something difficult and you just don't have a lot of energy or capacity? What happens when our inner resources are needed in other areas of our lives? Or, what if our bodies change or our hormones fluctuate, or we lose a family member or a beloved pet, and there is no capacity for anything *but* surviving?

Where's the inspiration then? You can't DO inspired action when you aren't inspired and your capacity has been reduced to zero. And how the hell does inspired action work for people struggling in systemic oppression. I see now that inspiration is mostly accessible when our nervous systems are regulated and our primary needs are met. That's where the wheels fell off in the "Inspired Action Only" mantra for me.

With physical capacity tapped out, and a fried nervous system I began to experiment with something different in my life and work.

With my desire for sustainability, slow, and steady, I experimented with creating and cultivating simple, sustainable, and nourishing habits that made sense for me and my business. I looked at everything that was heavy and burdensome in my life. I considered any and everything that wasn't simple. What wasn't supportive had to go. I sold my enormous historic house (those come with constant repairs and maintenance) and I downsized my home and my finances. In my business, I stopped offering nine different programs and I doubled down on creating a simple community coaching membership program for my clients. For two and a half years, I sold nothing but my coaching membership — *one* thing.

As I healed, my inspiration and capacity were puny for a few years. I gave myself softness emotionally, and simplicity in the tactics of living and working. I committed to the experiment of seeing what would happen in my business if I focused on just one thing for an extended period of time. I wondered, what would happen if I slowed down my life and my habits? Could slow really be fast? Could slow really be smooth?

To be in service, of simply one thing, didn't mean I only *did* one thing, it wasn't *that* simple. I did make a commitment to say yes only to elements of work that were in service to that one thing. I began to ask myself what habits and nourishing practices would really serve this new model, too.

The habits that create sustainability in your business often seem boring. To inspired action zealots, boring equals uninspired on the surface, but it doesn't have to be. What if I created daily habits and rituals that served my one offering, but also left me feeling inspired and physically capable? I began to see that the mundane could be the miracle in my life and work. Being willing to *do* and *be* the boring could be the biggest blessing to my business.

I was right.

Another distinction I had to make during this adjustment was: inspiration versus intuition. I get inspired ideas often. It's really important, as a soulful business owner, to slow down enough to evaluate whether our ideas are something to take action on, or something to put in the metaphorical crock pot to marinate for a while. Slowing down might mean five minutes, it doesn't have to mean three weeks. Slowing down means pausing and checking in from my center. Slowing down, for me, means calm, conscious breathing, and coming from my core SELF as a way of being, not just as a response to stress. I had to cultivate daily habits that made space for pause, so that I could hear my intuition and inner wisdom around my inspired ideas.

Today, I call these habits nourishing practices. Some of mine include:

- ♥ a slow, but forward moving tempo in all things. I call this "Slow Tango"

- ♥ daily movement = walking or rowing

- ♥ taking my supplements and meds as directed, and at the proper times

- ♥ lots of water

- ♥ intentional breathing

- ♥ daily reading

- ♥ daily writing

- ♥ daily journaling and parts work

- ♥ regular space for creativity and art

- ♥ space between appointments in my calendar

- ♥ no appointments before 10:00 a.m.

- ♡ my skincare and makeup routines combined with saying kind things to myself in the mirror

- ♡ stretching my hips before bed

- ♡ time outside with the sun in my face and my feet on the ground

- ♡ profit first Fridays with my bank accounts; being with my finances and allocating money to the appropriate accounts each week

- ♡ Sunday evening ME time in my office

Yes, this is a long-ass list. It didn't all happen at once. I was intentional and cultivated, one nourishing practice at a time. It is now the way I BE with myself in the world. I say "no" to so *much* so I can say yes to these things. It works for me at t̸ ̸ ̸age of my life and work. It gives me the energy to also prac̸ ̸ ̸ ̸ ̸ ̸ ̸n my business that create connection, clients, and i̸

No amount of money ̸ ̸ ̸ ̸ ̸ ̸ ̸ ̸ ̸ ̸ng changed my financial mess. Religio̸ ̸ ̸ ̸ ̸ ̸ ̸ ̸ ̸ ̸ ̸d SOPs (standard operating proce̸ ̸ ̸ ̸ ̸ ̸ ̸ ̸ ̸ ̸ ̸ ̸ys pay my taxes on time and in fu̸ ̸ ̸ ̸ ̸ ̸ ̸ ̸etirement, and get my insurance, will,̸ ̸ ̸ ̸ ̸ ̸ ̸ ̸nd advanced directives in order. Who kn̸ ̸ ̸ ̸ ̸ ̸ ̸ ̸erating instead of a mental burden?

You want freedom? Free̸ ̸ ̸ ̸ ̸ ̸ ̸ ̸ ̸ ̸spontaneity or inspiration — it's cultivated through your habits and nourishing practices. It's compounded through boring practice. I love inspiration, but you can't build a sustainable life and career on dopamine hits.

Here's a bonus tip: create habits that DO provide you with healthy dopamine hits, so you don't find yourself wanting. I use hobbies, and I give myself full permission to try new things to satisfy my needs for something fresh and new. New art supplies and new books are fabulous dopamine hits for me, and they don't require me to go into a deficit of cash or energy.

My habits are aligned with my values. The habits *you* cultivate, though, need to support you and only you. There is a lot of noise out there around tracking your habits. You could track ten habits every day if you wanted to, but how would that serve you, your health, and the health of your business? I don't want to just "do" a habit for the sake of "doing" a habit. I want to cultivate the nourishing practices and habits that create a sustainable and joyful life in the direction of my personalized dreams and my own, unique definition of success.

What questions could you answer for yourself that would really support your specific personality, climate, and desires?

Until I was in my forties, I'd never had to consider my physical vitality and health, and ultimately I had to ask myself, "What will create sustainable and long-term health, vitality, and physical capacity for my life and my business? What cultivated habits will be a fulcrum for me? What practices will help me to nurture my energy and my inspiration and all of my other strengths? What habits and unconscious practices are sucking the life out of my desired way of being and doing?"

Recently I was diagnosed with ADHD, and I realized that my brain functions very differently than what the world expects and demands. This diagnosis and the education around ADHD, especially the way ADHD shows up in adult women, has relieved so much internal shame I had not realized I was carrying.

Since my diagnosis and working with my doctors (my ADHD doc, my bioidentical hormone doc, and my therapist), I've set boundaries, made accommodations, and created standard operating procedures and nourishing practices in my life and work that support the way my neurodiverse brain works. One of the biggest thieves of my energy and capacity was mental load, and open mental loops. I didn't realize how much the mental stimulation weighed on my physical system. Overthinking is exhausting, literally. The relief I now live in is *real*. My capacity has increased, shame is non-existent, and it is so much easier to be in the boredom of my beautiful, sustaining nourishing practices.

Turns out some of the capacity and sustainability struggles that were affecting my life and business weren't just a "mindset" thing. Please don't try to meditate, or use Neuro Linguistic programming, or even exercise and diet your way to better physical and mental health. Get well-rounded, age-related, support from trusted professionals.

Wouldn't it be nice if it could be "hacked?" It can't — you are too unique and organic — you aren't a machine.

# Give Yourself Accessible SOPs

As I learn more about my neurodivergence, I can see how much the world and its typical systems are built for neurotypical people. When you think differently, doing things in traditional or typical fashion can backfire, because when it doesn't work we can internalize the failure instead of seeing the system failures. It's called "masking" when a person with a neurodiverse brain makes themself fit into a neurotypical system in order to be accepted or fit in.

ADHD or not, each of us is unique, and if something isn't working for you, rather than taking on the failure, we can cultivate alternative ways of being and doing — accessible *standard operating procedures* — that support us toward the means we seek to create.

Here's an example of one of my accessible SOPs:

While I incessantly write things down, including to-do lists, to-do lists don't really work for me. They can create more mental load and overwhelm, which can, if unchecked, lead to shame and TILT in my nervous system. The micro-details of a to-do list, or any kind of bullet-point-seven-step-system, tend to overwhelm me, because they restrict my need for space, creativity, and circular thinking.

I've discovered I don't need a traditional system or routine or a calendar scheduled to the hilt. What works for me are calendar *containers* that have a directional essence.

Containers + Intentional Essence
= FLOW = GET IT DONE!

As an example, here are the first two calendar containers of my day:

WAKE ♥ UP ♥ CONTAINER
(approx 5:30 am – 7:45 AM)

ESSENCE OF ATTENTION: dogs & gentle easing into the day.

USUALLY INVOLVES: I pee ♥ take meds ♥ dogs pee dogs meds ♥ dogs food ♥ coffee for me ♥ TV ON – LOCAL NEWS or GMA ♥ Phone in my Hand Scrolling SOCIALS ♥ outside time w dogs ♥ inside time w dogs ♥ maybe a walk ♥ maybe Re-rack.

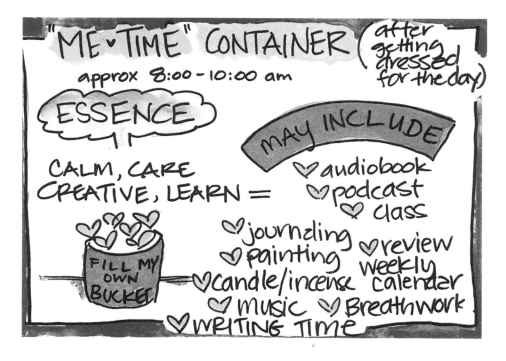

"ME ♥ TIME" CONTAINER (after getting dressed for the day)
approx 8:00 – 10:00 am

ESSENCE

CALM, CARE CREATIVE, LEARN =

FILL MY OWN BUCKET

MAY INCLUDE
♥ audiobook
♥ podcast
♥ class
♥ journaling ♥ review weekly calendar
♥ painting
♥ candle/incense
♥ music ♥ Breathwork
♥ WRITING TIME

A few of my other containers are:

- Client Service
- Financials
- Sunday Evening Planning
- Business Planning
- Rest/Play

My calendar isn't scheduled to the hilt. I am intentionally a homebody and very rarely do social things outside of the house. I protect my space and "me" time as sacred and necessary. I say no to so much. My nervous system needs space. When I agree to doing something, it must be aligned with my being and my values, and doable for my nervous system.

It took me years to create the containers that work for me, and they can shift depending on the needs of my family, dogs, and other life circumstances. These days I am an empty nester, therefore, the demands of kid's schedules and needs are no longer taking up space in my everydays. My business isn't new and I am already proficient in the fundamental skills I need to make my life and business work. Both my life context and my values will probably differ from yours, so, if this sparks possibility for you, make your own custom containers according to the essence, task, and lifestyle important to you.

Space, with defined edges and an intentional essence, helps my flow kick in. When I am in flow — you guessed it — I always accomplish my tasks. It doesn't always appear as though I expect it to. My accomplishments in flow usually resemble a butterfly or a bumble bee — I'm rarely flying in a linear direction.

What I have come to learn and understand on my ADHD journey is that ADHD is about executive functioning.

When my brain is presented with too much detail
= no ability to make a decision.

When my brain is presented with too broad or too vague = no ability to make a decision.

Space, with a themed "container" and the energy/ essence of _____ = success for me.

For example: From 8:00 a.m. to 11:00 a.m. is "me-time" with the essence and energy of calm, creativity, and expression = success.

Before I realized this process and way of being was normal and effective for me, I was always attempting to make myself fit in the world's standard operating procedures. This led to frustration and exasperation because of the shame stories in my head. Here are a couple that took up residence often: "I can't plan, or follow a schedule." Also, "Something is wrong with me." Or the ever-present, "I'm doing it wrong." These stories lived in my every days — heavy, like a thick, wet blanket dragging me down, leaving me feeling tired. My diagnosis and recognition around the simple truth of the ways that I uniquely thrive gave me the final permission to do things the dang way that works for me.

You don't need a diagnosis to find a personal system that works for you. You know you better than anyone, and you know what you need in order to feel balanced and aligned. Nothing is wrong with you. You trust you! What elements help you get to flow — that's the plan. The "to-do list" will get done once we are in our desired essence, but focusing on the to-do list before flow fucks us *up*. Get in alignment and *then*.

I encourage 80 percent of our time to be spent meandering our way to a relaxed and calm nervous system, building up to a flow state; once we're in it, everything gets done in that remaining 20 percent of the time, because calm, flow, and the following hyperfocus always get you to your goal. Not only that, it feels good in the process of getting there along the way.

Your way may not make sense to the world, just as my way doesn't make sense to neurotypical people, but it makes sense to us. We just gotta be willing to do it our way and release the "you are doing it wrong" stories we've carried for a lifetime.

PS: Thank you to my client KR for bringing such a great question to our group coaching call — my flow of brilliant ideas is often created from the connection with clients through conversation. None of us are alone. If you have, or think you might have ADHD, or love someone who you think/does, I find it so helpful to not just know about ADHD (and any neurodivergent brains), but to understand how an ADHD brain functions. Learn about it. It can make a difference.

# I Didn't Want to Believe It, But It's True

For most of my life the word *habits* made me cringe. I made up in my mind that those habits were constricting and limiting my spunk and freedom. When I picked up James Clear's book *Atomic Habits*[3] I fell in love with the concept he presented at the beginning of the book: your habits are an embodiment of your identity. I relate to I AM — to my being — those terms are my jam, and like an "I coulda had a V-8" moment, it smacked me in the head as so *true*.

When I think about what I want to create in my business and how I want to impact the world, I also need to consider who I am, who I want to become, and also, who am I *not being* right now? How does my being have to change in order for me to become the person I want to be in this world?

My being, my identity, subconsciously shows up in my habits. I consciously show up in my behaviors and the doing in my life.

What habits are engaged by a person who is able to finish a book? What processes does she put in place? Completing a book sounds difficult, but does writing today for thirty minutes sound hard? Does the process of writing consistently sound hard? Sometimes yes, and sometimes no. But, I *know* I can do hard things. I used to be the one who only wanted to do the fun things; I didn't want to do the boring things. Once upon a time, I didn't want to look at the resistance. Now, however, I have a kind of counterbalance, and that was born out of the habits I started years ago.

The habits that I started back then have just become my way of being, the way I move around the world. These habits are so boring right now that they aren't even fun to talk about anymore. But I do them most every day, because they matter, and because they are attached to the identity of the person I am and the person I want to be in the world.

Here's an example: let's talk about making a living as an artist. If you want to make a living as an artist, you must make art but you also must *sell* your art. Making art is inspiring and allows you to feel creative and in flow. Selling art, on the other hand, might feel boring, hard, and repetitive.

When we make art, we're doing that from our inspiration. Yay inspiration! But if you want to make a living at it, you have to do some of the mundane stuff, so that you can access the complete magic. I want you to honor your inspiration, but I also encourage you to check your inspiration. A lot of people live through inspiration only, which doesn't always give them the opportunity to feel the completeness of creative magic and its entire process.

We all have a need for some excitement and novelty at times, but that doesn't have to come at the expense of your process and habits. What if you were willing to be boring *and* bored by your processes and your habits. My business is both exciting and boring, and because of this, it is both sustainable and supportive.

Nurturing practices for life and business are what actually create sustainable results. It's easy and sexy to focus on achievements, outcomes, and goals. You can see and desire the vision, the goal, but if you aren't committed to the process and the practice, your vision won't become the reality. Sustainability comes from practices, habits, and processes in all areas: body, nervous system, emotional self, thinking self, spirit, business marketing and selling, and finances and money.

You've imagined that BEING and the vision will just happen, like manna coming down from heaven, if you just *think* about it enough. Nope. You gotta build the internal capacity and commit to the nourishing practices.

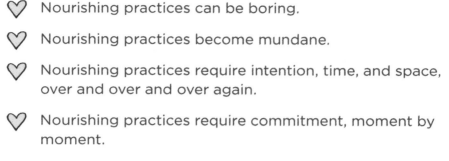 Nourishing practices can be boring.

 Nourishing practices become mundane.

Nourishing practices require intention, time, and space, over and over and over again.

Nourishing practices require commitment, moment by moment.

Nourishing practices require years, yes years, of time on task.

Your BEING can't be bought on Amazon Prime.

CULTIVATE your nourishing practices over time.

The more you cultivate, the more these practices create a subconscious muscle memory. And the more that happens, the less effort the practices require, the less mental load you carry. This means less exhaustion and overwhelm. Consistent effort and practice is what will produce the ease you crave. You can want it fast all day, or you can calmly and clearly decide to *slow* down.

What do you want to create and who do you need to be in order to create it? What are the practices that will bring you to that place? Some days this process of becoming is exciting. Many moments are excruciating and itchy. What I offer is never a demand, or even a request. It is only ever an invitation to inquire within, and to practice.

# I Am . . .

Calm

Connected

Compassionate

Curious

Confident

Creative

Clear

Courageous

I am a woman of range. I am all of these and . . .

I AM GRUMPY.

And ya know what? I'm not mad about it. Why? Because under my grumps and irritation are:

Desire

Pain

Grief

Sadness

Despite conditioning and culture that shames these states of mind and feeling, irritations and grumps are an invitation to actually *live human*. They are an invitation to feel it all — the sensations in your body — let them be

noticed,

felt,

held . . .

with tender compassion.

I will not leave these feelings and sensations in my body to rot, to war, and to create disease.

I will create holy space for all my feelings, all parts of me. I will bring them into the warm love of my presence. I will hear their voices. And I will breathe connection and curiosity into each of them.

Hello Grumpy. I am with you. And I love us.

# A Place Where Mainline Personal Development Falls Short

Alright, friends — I need you to know something really important: like *know* it down to your core.

First, let me say that I love coaching. I love soul-full, transformational coaching. I love anchoring into self-leadership. I love self-development — I always have. I even love . . . wait for it . . . sales. But, it's time to call bullshit. There is one particular concept in the mainline personal growth world that is tossed around as truth, when in reality, there is so much more nuance to the truth.

When in doubt I always think it's a good idea to come back to the basics. However, sometimes the basics are the very things that lead us astray. There is an inherent premise — or basic — in the self-development world that gets us all into trouble and accounts for much of the misery we experience.

Here it is: There are positive emotions and there are negative emotions, and you want to get rid of all the negative ones if you are going to have a happy and successful life.

Every time I see someone spouting a variation of the idea that emotions are negative, I just want to reach out and smack 'em. I know these people are coming with an intention to help, and at first, it feels good, but this idea is harmful. There is no such thing as negative emotions. If you haven't heard this truth bomb before, prepare to have your mind blown. Are you ready?

Emotions are *neutral.*

Believing that there are "good" emotions and "bad" emotions — that some are "positive" and some are "negative" — sets us up to be on a hamster wheel of suffering. This idea teaches us a couple of things.

In order to become whole and "happy," we need to slam through mental and emotional difficulties instead of meeting and caring for the emotions as they show up. When we position certain emotions as negative, we inadvertently create shame and blame around experiencing the range of normal human emotions.

This is a concept that isn't just hyped in personal development circles. It's perpetuated everywhere. And it runs deep. It induces shame and moral judgment on your humanness. Yes, some emotions are pleasant, and many are uncomfortable, but not negative.

There are a lot of things my dad taught me when I was growing up. Some of these things he learned from his father before him, and so on. As an adult, what I notice is that the men in my family don't handle emotion very well, especially from women. As a child, I often heard "stop that crying bullshit," and I was expected to just turn the tears and the emotion off. At the time, I didn't understand, but I internalized that the crying and the emotions associated with the crying were "bad." I was "bad."

As an adult, I now understand what is behind this need to eradicate the "bad" emotions, but honestly, it has taken me a long time. I didn't understand it as a twenty-year-old. I didn't understand it as a thirty-year-old. My work around this, my insights, and my wide openness did not come until my shoved-down emotions were so thick that I had no other choice than to allow them to be felt. Those pressed-down emotions affected not only my emotional state but my physical health as well.

During this time when my physical health was compromised, I was doing expressive arts training with Chris Zydel (she is the wise mentor who held me in the first story in this book). Up until this point, no matter how many times I had heard people speak about "meeting your discomfort," I never really understood it. This is because, for years I was either *depressing* down my emotions (which caused depression) or the opposite, *thinking* my emotions (which caused anxiety). I had no concept for how to *meet* my discomfort. I did not know how to feel the sensations of my emotions, let alone meet them. This spectrum from depressing down my emotions on one end to the chaos of thinking my emotions on the other end didn't provide a path for me to actually *feel* my discomfort somatically — in my body. Now I know that meeting my discomfort lies in the middle of this spectrum.

This concept in the personal development world — that we have to overcome negative emotions — is definitely not the path of meeting the discomfort. Striving to overcome your negative emotions is a great short-term strategy that feels really good in the moment. It also happens to bypass both the learning and the potential for expansion and increased mental and physical capacity for emotions as well.

Our emotions are a gift, sensations indicating data from our miraculous biology. Our emotions have vital information for us, if we can learn to be with them in our bodies, and listen. Many emotions are caused by our thoughts. In traditional personal development and coaching models, programming equals thoughts, thoughts cause feelings, feelings dictate your actions, and your actions dictate your results. I teach a lot from that model, I understand it. It's a good starting point. And, here is the nuanced difference: the circumstances that ignite this process are neutral, just as emotions are neutral. These circumstances give rise to our thoughts. These thoughts absolutely impact our feelings and sensations. And instead of just changing the thought to bypass and create a new feeling, I've learned that meeting those feelings, meeting those emotions, recognizing the sensations, listening to your body and what it wants to teach us, has been very valuable and helpful. And it doesn't leave our emotions pressed into the recesses of our bodies to explode on someone down the road.

To simply "change your thought" can be violent to our inner systems. There are only two places we can go with this when we try to bypass and overcome emotions with a simple thought change. When we notice emotions arise, we can froth them into drama, or we can mute them and smack a new thought over them, hoping for change. Neither one of those options are helpful in the long game.

When we meet our emotions, we acknowledge them and notice them. We can distinguish between the thought that causes the emotion, and the physical sensation in our bodies. As if they are their own personality, we can ask these parts of us what they're here to teach us. Are the emotions here to teach us something that is real and true, and needs to be honored? If so, how can we allow for that? How do we surrender to it? How do we embrace it? Is there something to be attended to, witnessed, healed, expressed? Do these emotions point to old, old stories that live in our bones and DNA, or do they contain present circumstance information for us?

> There, there, Fear.
> I see you, I hear you.
> I am here for you,
> I will not leave you.
> What do you want me to know?

If the emotions are not here to teach us, if they are merely an exercise in catastrophe, drama, or frothing, how do we nurture the discomfort and begin to cultivate new experiences without bypassing the emotions?

Another way I approach meeting the discomfort, is asking whether it is useful or not. I remember being in a workshop once where we were discussing this concept, and there was an older couple sitting next to me that had just lost their granddaughter to the flu. It was a devastating loss. They were trying to reconcile the concept that circumstances are neutral. Was the circumstance of this death neutral? Could they just choose a different thought? This death had just happened two weeks prior to the workshop. They were grieving. We don't want to bypass that grief by transforming it into something else in that moment (or trying to). Would it have been useful to do something other than grieve in that moment? I can't answer that for anyone, but for that moment and that couple, their grief was a useful emotion. It was not "negative."

A woman once asked me, "But what if someone is abusive to you? Isn't that a negative emotion?" Please note that emotion and behavior are two different things. *Feeling* anger doesn't have to be harmful to one's self or to another. *Behavior* out of anger can certainly be negative and harmful.

Sometimes anger is a useful emotion, and sometimes anger is not. Often, we use anger to bypass. I've learned that when my anger burns hot, there are fears and desires that need to be tended to — deeper in my system. Sometimes my anger feels violent. I have angry parts that want to cuss and cut and harm. When I get curious with these parts, I connect with compassion and presence, and they soften and let me know what is really going on. The anger is easier to feel than the pain. It fills the hole we want to avoid.

Look around at all the obvious things people do to avoid difficult feelings. There are Twelve Step programs for all of them. And, some of us can be super sneaky and use behaviors that are completely acceptable in society to mask the pain.

Yes, drinking away your pain is alcoholism, but what about being ruthlessly "positive," or taking personal growth course after course, to avoid feeling what hurts inside? How about that Amazon "BUY NOW" button? Busyness, or working non-stop? What about taking care of everyone around you and ignoring your own needs?

Can you imagine what it would be like if we were able to learn how to move toward, meet, and process our emotions — all of them, the full spectrum of them — when we were children instead of in our middle-aged life? What would that be like?

UNARMORED

And so, I invite you to take a pause when you come to the place of processing your thoughts, feelings, and actions. If you find a thought or a sensation that feels uncomfortable, instead of just running right through it and switching things up, let's *pause* for a moment and breathe. Let's take an inventory, take responsibility, inquire compassionately within, and notice what needs to happen. And then, when we're complete with meeting the feelings, which sometimes can happen quickly, and sometimes may take a little while, *then* we can move on to a more useful thought, a more useful emotion, and a more useful action.

# Fire Ants,
# Embodied Emotions

My mental capacity has always been a primary leader in my life. I love to think. I love to learn. I love to process. I love to be in my head. I love my thinking self. I give her so much credit. I tell her all the time how fucking smart she is. On the flip side, I'm not very good with being in my body. I get antsy and squirmy at even the thought of dancing.

For most of my life, being in my head, being in my learning and strategic parts, and being in my thinking has solved a lot of problems for me. My thinking has created money and jobs. It has helped me heal. I'm sure it saved me, somehow, from things that I didn't even realize when I was a little kid. I notice that a lot of my clients are similar to me. They're really smart people and they are very effective in a strategic and cognitive world. Often, they are also really cut off from their bodies. I can relate.

I have a couple of good friends who are big embodiment people, and they used to make me so nervous the same way dancing does. Making art is usually the way I connect my head to my body. My personal portal to embodiment is painting. When I started painting in my forties, it was the beginning of me understanding my emotions outside of my intellect. Painting, for me, is a full-body experience. It requires big movements, and I like working on big canvas.

Even though I have a connection to embodiment through painting, I still need reminders to help me tune into my body and stop relying so much on my intellect. And that's how these fucking fire ants made their way into my life.

I was at my friend Laura's house for girls' night a couple of months ago, and I parked in her driveway. The next day I had ants everywhere inside my beloved truck — and not just any little ants, these were fire ants. Apparently, if you park on an ant hill, they will relocate into or onto whatever disrupts their home. Who knew? It took me about a week to fully get the ants out of my truck (hint if your car is ever covered in fire ants: that little pressured air blower from the carwash is super helpful).

A few weeks later, I had some conflict experiences, or rather my parts created an experience of conflict with various coaches and leaders in my life. Some of my parts just didn't want me to feel my feelings — they were being really stubborn, and I could almost hear them admonishing me, "Don't go there. If you feel this, you will die. If you feel this, you will be left."

I was really angry. And my husband happened to be going through some difficult stuff, too. My husband is a retired teacher and now has a podcast that is called, *I'm Not Mad, I'm Just Irritated*. Basically, he gets paid for complaining on his podcast. His schtick is: my life is garbage. And of course, I can't stand it when he says that. I can't stand it when he complains. Why can't I stand it when he complains? Because I haven't *allowed myself* to complain. I'm the one following some made-up rule that complaining is garbage.

So, one Friday, I've just gotten off a call, and I am irritated as fuck. I decided that I needed to release and vent some of this anger, and I also decided to bring Mr. Complainer along for the ride. We drove out to the lake by our house and parked the truck, got out, and leaned on the tailgate. He was angry, and I was angry. We weren't angry at each other, but we were both angry. Sensing the freedom of the open area around us, I suggested, "Hey, let's yell at the sky and the lake: My life is garbage!"

He just looked at me like I'm fucking nuts, y'all.

I didn't care if he thought I was nuts so I just started yelling, "My life is garbage. This inner work is hard!" I let my boiling anger flow over and release. Louder and louder, from the inside of my being and then out into the sky, I released my anger and energy into a controlled space — not directed at anyone — just to the sky and the water in front of me.

Then, at my feet, I felt a searing sting. I looked down and my fluorescent, multicolored ASICs and my socks were covered in fire ants. And they were fucking stinging me! I was standing in a lakeside fire ant mound. Seriously, are you kidding me? Again with the fire ants!

I instinctively started stomping and moving my whole body. I flapped and slapped, doing my best to brush off the fire ants with my hands. I was madly shaking my feet, moving as fast as I could in a desperate attempt to escape the stings. I stripped my shoes and socks off, and eventually my pants. (Fire ants in your pants is not something anyone wants to experience.) There I stood, on the side of the big blue lake under the open sky, half naked, and hopping around like a wild jumping bean, all because of my anger and the fire ants.

It took weeks for the bites from those damn fire ants to heal. It probably took almost as long for that rage of mine to die down, too. As I reflected on all this, I began to think about what these fire ants were trying to teach me. My first reaction to that reflection was: NOTHING! The residue of my irritation, both emotionally and physically, was clearly still present. Then, I slowed down, took a slow, deep breath, and asked my parts what they needed. Those parts that were angry and defiant and stubborn.

My depression said, "Allison, you have grief, you actually need to cry out, you need to feel it."

And my anger wisely said, "Allison, we are clogged with emotion. You need to feel and you need to stomp into the ground."

Those fire ants taught me something that changed my whole fucking life. When the fire ants were biting, I needed to move in order to get them off my body. For me, the anger and frustration I was feeling was just like those damn ants.

I knew I needed to move that energy out of my body. I don't have a consistent "movement practice." Some people have beautiful movement practices for the sole purpose of releasing energy and emotion. They're so good at it. Not me. I'm a newbie. And so I walked. And on my walk, I gave myself permission to consciously complain. I verbally released my salty words, and I allowed each step to be a punching bag, discharging the anger and frustration.

After that walk, I felt more at ease. I went back and debriefed my own experience. How did I clear that up so fast? Wouldn't it be nice if I could move through my emotions like that in the future? After I moved those emotions through me, I experienced a lot of vitality and flow and clarity that I'd been missing. When you unclog the pipes, and release the debris, the water can flow.

My body reminds me of the fire ants again. It reminds me that when we hit fire ants, we can use our whole body to shake or brush away the pain. It is futile to sit in our heads and intellectualize; and in these moments, any kind of seven-step plan is a fucking joke. Overthinking won't get you out of the fire ant pile. If you're in fire ants or a swarm of bees, you instinctively start using your whole being to move. The body knows.

The fire ant experience helped me see that I had a lot of anger that needed to be wisely and usefully discharged. Sometimes there's obvious grief that we need to work and move through, and then sometimes we just hit a seemingly arbitrary puddle of grief. My nature in the past has been to rationalize, coach, intellectualize, or even try to comprehend the grief, but that's all from the neck up. The fire ants were a real life affirmation that my body needs more of me, my body is calling me to wholeness. No more simply being head-led.

I'm learning to move toward anger, move toward grief, move toward disappointment, and move toward various uncomfortable emotions. Instead of pushing them away, I'm learning to gather information and create relationships with them. I'm learning not only to *think* these emotions but also to work with my body and to intentionally have sessions of feeling them. It's working.

I tell myself a lot of stories. My emotions are telling me, "Allison, I use these stories to get your attention so that you'll drop into our body and notice the sensations in your body. Pay attention to these sensations. Slow down. Listen. I am using these stories to let you know what you need to move through *with your body*."

The double dose of fire ants gave me an invitation to a new relationship with my emotions and with my body. I invite you to begin a relationship with your emotions, too, and not just in your head. Notice sensations. Gather information. Discharge the energy that accumulates with the emotions that build up. Hopefully, you won't have to endure fire ants biting your ankles or approaching your coochie.

Many people are experiencing clogged pipes and constipated emotions. It's how we've been conditioned. It's not a problem that needs to be solved, but rather than waiting for the pipe to burst, maybe we could all learn to unclog a little bit through somatic body and movement practices.

# Move Toward

For a long time when I was experiencing depression, I ignored it. The mantra I used daily to try and self-soothe until the depression lifted sounded something like, "Oh, it'll go away, the flow always comes back."

One day, instead of hoping for it to go away, I turned my ear toward Depression with an open and compassionate heart. As I listened, I heard Depression say, "Could you please come and visit with me? I have wisdom to share with you."

I listened and learned, "You do have deep and insightful wisdom for me."

Since it had my attention, Depression continued, "Yes, I have some grief. And I don't want you just to think about what you're grieving. I want you to move and flail and cry, and complain. I want you to move this all through you and out of you. I want you to do this consciously — as a choice — in a safe space without harming anyone else. I need you to be determined to move like you were determined with the fire ants. This sting is just as painful and will last longer if you ignore it."

I heard what Depression had to say, and I moved as it asked me to move. What if, when the emotions came, I could meet them, connect with them, listen to them, nourish them, and move with them?

Contrast, disappointment, irritation, not getting what you want, frustration, rage, even grief — these are the most GLORIOUS teachers IF you will inquire within, compassionately and gently, when they come up. Social conditioning misled you into running away from these wise parts of you. But when you, instead, turn toward them, they will show you the *clear true wonderful you*. Seared to the depths of your SOUL, the radiance of YOU.

Other people won't get it. They won't understand that your complaints may be conscious and held in power, not held in victimhood.

But you cannot bypass it. You cannot shove it down, or leave it in your body. You must move toward it with calm and care and curious love. There will be a time when you simply know you *must*. In order to reveal the true you, to build the trust and connections you long for, it will become the thing you can't *not* do — meeting all of you.

All these parts, hidden by the good girl, the behaved ones, the polite and refined, the parts of you that yearn to be pleasing . . . they need to be connected with you. They need to be safely embodied. Brush it out, stomp it into the earth, yell it to the sky. The earth beneath you can hold it. The water around you can hold it. Give it to the wind and the sky.

# The Landslides that Brought Me Down

You know the song. Let it play in your head, *Fleetwood Mac*, or maybe the version by *The Chicks*.

Ok . . . so it was more like a *landmine*, or a series of them.

A lifetime of shoving shit down will do that . . . create an internal compression bomb in your being that can only explode in the most inopportune moments. Wouldn't it be nice if we could anticipate the explosion and take it to the lake and stomp it out before it detonates, leaving its emotional, mental, and relationship carnage?

For me, these landmine experiences didn't involve rational emotional responses, the stimulus didn't warrant the response that came out of me. No matter what I knew in my head, I could not soothe the intense emotional pain. These episodes blew me to bits.

For most of my adult life, I have had these *mostly* private landmine emotional episodes. I suppose I kind of expected them in my youth and in dumb relationships with boys, but as I grew in my own emotional intelligence, wisdom, and in my "mindset skills," I guess I thought they would lessen. When these episodes would still rise up in me from time to time, literally flooding my entire body with dread and fear and the sense of being four years old again, the shame hangover and mental war in my head would last for months.

What made it worse? The events that seemed to lead up to these experiences weren't with my beloveds. They weren't with people that mattered deeply to me. They were often in business relationships, some with horrible bosses, some with shitty colleagues, and one with a service provider. The time that passed between "shitty colleague incident" and "service provider incident" (yes, I remember every single one) was the longest ever. I'd almost thought I'd finally healed.

I needed to pause a marketing contract. Having completed the initial year agreement and now on a month-to-month work agreement, my intuition told me to take a three-month break, not just from the contract, but from all marketing. My business was shifting and I needed clarity before spending money in an outdated direction. It was a $2,300 per month expense for my business. I called the provider directly, to have a voice-to-voice conversation about my options for pausing.

What had always been a friendly and cooperative working relationship, for me, instantly felt ice cold. I hadn't expected the tenor of her verbal and energetic response at all, and in a moment there were a handful of parts within me that took over my being and that phone call.

Mostly present there, on the phone, was the little girl who felt criticized and rejected out of the blue, like she'd done something horribly wrong. The tears started streaming and nothing in me could stop them.

Other parts of me were horrified, because I was now "little-girling" on the phone with this person.

The diplomatic, boundaried, negotiator, self-advocate, and business owner, who maintained amicable neutrality in difficult conversations, was there, but it was as if she was behind a three-foot plexiglass wall, watching in horror, unable to retract the conversation.

Fuuuuuuuccccckkkkkk . . .

It was my meltdown in this conversation that resulted in my reaching out to a colleague for a therapist referral. This was something coaching hadn't fixed in fifteen years. It was time to try something new. My colleague, with thirty years of experience as a therapist, and now a leadership coach, took me on as a client just before my forty-ninth birthday, and she sent me a few books. Coaches always send books. But this book was a portal to a practice and way of seeing the world, my world, that changed everything.

When I began reading the first two pages of *Introduction to the Internal Family Systems Model*[4] by Richard C. Schwartz, one of the books my new coach gave me, it made so much intellectual sense, *and* my body felt a softness and release of tension I didn't even realize I had lifted. My curiosity about this work was both intellectually and somatically ignited.

In traditional coach training, we are taught about inner critics, the inner child, the ways we outsource discomfort and avoid taking action, and other inner personalities. The directional nature of coaching lends itself to this "fixing and overcoming" and of these parts. Yes, we are taught curious questioning skills, but this had softness, presence, something different.

My body instinctively leaned in with a knowing that this was a direction that would hold me. Parts that had always been shoved away, were relaxed, felt welcome, and were intrigued. This work gave me a path to a connected relationship with these parts. Just two pages and I was all in.

# Is It an Itch or Is It Flow?

Here's a distinction I'd like to present for your Soul-full consideration:

- Does your desire to take action come from discomfort or an innate creative drive?
- The discomfort is itchy and agitated. The itch is dehydrated, thirsty, and scratchy.
- Innate creative drive feels different. It almost feels as though it moves of its own accord. It flows.
- Flow is supple, emergent on its own, and overflowing.
- Is your expression from performance and thirst, or is it pure creativity, unleashed in divine timing?

I see lots of itching people lately. It's predictable, right? If you are looking, it's as cyclical as the seasons: Notice when the cozy dormancy of winter has worn off but spring is not yet here. You are the same. What's in you may be resting just beneath the surface, but not yet ready to bloom. We can't rush the seasons.

Let it rest. Let yourself rest.

Settle into the waiting with your presence.

The flow always comes back.

# PSA

Just a loving reminder:

More is not better. Better is better.

# PART 2

# Connection

# BE Yourself

What the fuck does that mean? Seriously. I've been declaring that for myself and others for the last fifteen years, and I don't know shit about myself some days. Other days, I remember clearly. What I know every day is that I'm still peeling back layers to figure out what that means. Here's what else I know: That I do not know what "Be Yourself" means for you. So . . . *you* fill that in, here in this book.

PS. Date it. Perhaps, even, come back after reading each section of this brilliant book and answer the question for yourself, again and again, so you can see your conditioning fall away, the binding stitches come loose, and your TRUE SELF shine through.

*What the fuck does it mean to*
**BE YOURSELF?**

_____
_____
_____
_____
_____
_____
_____
_____
_____

Date: _____

# Why Is It So Hard to Be Yourself?

Why is it so hard for us to be our authentic selves? This is a question I have spent a lot of time thinking about and working on for myself. In my search for more exploration on this topic, I decided to enroll in a Compassionate Inquiry training class[5] with Gabor Maté, Ph.D. To my utter surprise and great delight, he shared the answer! The biological answer! THE ANSWER! Yes, that is a lot of exclamation points, and for me, life-long pondering of a question that receives an answer requires exclamation!

As a child I never considered the concept of authenticity. Only when I was pressed so hard and squeezed by the rules of my corporate job did I consider that I might not have to bear the emotional pain of the "rules" that contradicted my own care and values. As I began to step out in my own in work, I still felt myself bending in so many ways. The people-pleasing didn't stop when I quit my job; It was still there in my work, with my husband, and with my friends. It was still there, aching in my heart, living in my bones, and driving my behavior at the most inopportune times.

And then, Gabor Maté shared the most enlightening insight: As children we are born with two basic drives. The primary drive is for attachment — connection and to be cared for. The second is the drive for authenticity. He said when we are children and authenticity is held up in competition with attachment, attachment will win every time. In our class, Dr. Maté showed us a video of the "Still Face Experiment."[6] You can find it on YouTube — and beware, while it ends well, it can be emotional and triggering.

We already know that a baby who has all of their food and shelter needs provided can still die if they are not held and loved. In this experiment a mother is playing with her baby, just under a year old. She is connected and present for a while, engaging physically and emotionally. In the next phase of the experiment, she turns her head away quietly, and then back, with a "still face." There, but not present, no emotional connection — and it's horrifying to watch the baby's instant response to the disconnection.

The disconnection.

The baby's face and body change as she tries to re-engage her mother's connection. She begins the contorting process of trying and striving to find the energy of that connection. The baby tries to re-engage her mother with delight and smiles, and then screams and anger, and when no connection is restored, this little baby begins to hunch over, withdrawing into her body, shutting herself off, with tears coming quickly. And then, the mother re-engages, lights up and reconnects. The connection is restored and the baby is soothed.

When I show this video to my clients, most are viewing it through the lens of being an adult person, and they begin to feel protective of the baby. They view the experiment through the lens of a mother. From this lens, they project their judgment, naturally. It's a safe view of the video. Sometimes they see themselves as the mother, and flashes of shame and regret come over them for ways they think they may have hurt their own babies.

After a few moments of reflection, I ask them, with care, to try to see the experiment through the lens of the baby and to take notice of their own bodies and sensations.

When I first saw the video, I related to the baby, not the mom, perhaps because I'm mid-journey of sourcing all my own disconnection. As I viewed the video, I felt no fault of the mother. As the viewer we can see all the things our caretakers did wrong — intentionally or unintentionally, and I just wanted to be present to the baby's experience as a representation of my own. I made up a story of a mother who needs to pee as she's walking through the door with her baby in the car carrier. She sets it safely on the counter and runs to the bathroom, and for that moment the baby feels that disconnection. For a minute, I felt the sting and gasping of my own experiences of disconnection as a baby, a child, and an adult. Memories flashed through my mind where *I* had also been a disconnected mother unable to give a child, my pets, my own loved ones, my presence. Connection and disconnection, and the ways we adapt, went from being an intellectual concept to a somatic experience at that moment. Hundreds of moments came to my mind and rose to the awareness of my open heart. I saw and felt — of course, we bend and contort and *un-become* to maintain that connection.

I could see all the ways I still bend and contort and adapt unconsciously, so that I don't lose that coveted connection — my natural, innate need for connection and belonging. These parts of my personality were embedded as coping mechanisms long before I even heard the word "authentic." Our fear of losing our attachment, and that we won't be loved, drives *so much* of our personality, so we suppress our drive for attachment by disconnecting and rejecting ourselves.

I see it in me, I see it in the world around me. I see it in all the atrocities and injustices in the world . . . the disconnection.

Heavy, I know. But there is hope — great hope — and possibility.

Underneath all the bending and adaptations is our healthy and whole SELF. We, as adults, have the capacity to begin reconnecting with ourselves, and all the parts of us that have spent a lifetime bending to others in exchange for connection and love. We can begin to actually meet and befriend these parts of us that still exist in the shadows of our hearts and minds. We can learn to relate, connect with, and understand these parts that were only ever meant to protect us.

And when I say "we" here, I am really saying "I." *I* can see — I can see the seed of my discontent and the coping mechanisms, and if I can see, then I can gently unwind and re-cultivate with intention. I have been able to change old behavior, and release harmful patterns that no longer serve me. It's liberating, and light. When I experience that freedom and the healing that it brings, of course I want it for WE! Because I know you want it, too.

So, we can be authentic with ourselves *and* with the world around us, through connecting with ourselves first. Tender, compassionate SELF connection. The more I meet myself, the less I need the heavy armor. And that feels good.

# A Quick IFS (My Version of Parts Work) Primer for Context

Internal Family Systems (IFS)[7] is a modality that was developed in the therapy room by Dr. Richard S. Schwartz[8] over the last two and a half decades. Really, his clients helped him see the various elements of the framework, and now, IFS is used not only in therapy, but also in medicine, schools, business, and in coaching![9] It's also a helpful personal and spiritual practice for many.

Family therapists work with the "system of the family" — all the members of the family and how they relate to each other. Dr. Schwartz' work discovered that each person has an inner family system, and that we humans have a mind of multiplicity, not singularity.

Haven't we all said before, "A part of me feels XYZ, but another part of me knows ABC?"

The Internal Family System Model notes that there are four elements that make up our internal systems:

**A Central Core SELF** — SELF (and its energy) is the natural leader of your system and psyche, your natural essence, is undamaged, needs no improvement and is perfect as is. The SELF is the support and care you have always needed. It is the CORE YOU. This SELF is permeated with these eight Cs:

calm
connected
compassionate
curious
confident
creative
clear
courageous

**Exiles:** parts, often very young, that hold pain, trauma, rejection, deep wounds, and shame. These parts have been isolated, or "exiled" away, for their own protection. They are tender, vulnerable, and hold painful emotions, experiences, energies, and beliefs. Before their wounding, Exiles were full of eagerness, vitality, and innocence.

- Examples: not enough, fear of abandonment/rejection, too much, unlovable, shame, untethered, empty, worthlessness, undeserving.

**Protector Managers:** Managers run your daily life and give the illusion of control and safety. They are proactive, generally "acceptable," and use coping behaviors to prevent humiliation, rejection, and abandonment. They are dedicated to their jobs, but often exhausted and feel alone. Managers *never* want the system to feel the pain of the exiles again and are fiercely committed to their protective roles.

- Examples: people-pleasing, self-sabotage, anxiety, procrastination, excessive caretaking, overachieving, isolation, perfectionism.

**Protector Firefighters:** Firefighters are reactive parts who create diversions and prevent pain by numbing, bypassing, outsourcing, and distancing from difficult feelings. They claim they don't care about the consequences, and they often feel ashamed and isolated. Firefighters, also, never want the system to feel the pain of the exiles again.

- Examples: bypassing, eating disorders, addictions, substance abuse, anger issues, overspending, anything with the purpose of not feeling difficult emotions.

Exiles, Managers, and Firefighters carry pain and burdens, and the goal of this work is not to eliminate these parts, but to help them build trust in SELF energy and then release their burdens so they may serve updated roles in your system.

For example, perhaps you have people-pleasing parts (managers) that show up and "drive the bus" when the possibility of conflict arises in everyday life. Even though you "know better," you may find yourself fawning and caving in to avoid "making waves" in a relationship.

These protectors don't want you to feel the pain of conflict — or maybe they think they are preventing an exile from experiencing violence that happens if someone is unhappy or upset. When you were small, these protectors kept you safe from being smacked or yelled at by someone you loved (when you were little, disagreement sometimes meant rejection, isolation, anger or violence), and so over time these protectors took on this role to keep the little ones inside you from ever feeling that pain again.

Here are some of the important guiding principles of this work:

- IFS is non-pathologizing, inclusive, compassionate, spiritual, and deeply respectful, and provides us with inner authority.
- All parts have benevolent intent, no matter how problematic the behavior, and so we say "All Parts are Welcome" and use SELF energy and the 8C's to get to know and build trust and friendship with the parts.
- We remember that parts are all just trying to do what they think is best for us; they are only using coping strategies that made sense at one time, but are simply out of date now that we are adults. Curiously understanding parts, witnessing, and building trust are key to helping them adopt updated and more effective strategies.
- When interacting with parts, we respect their autonomy and reasons for what they are and are not willing to do. We respect that building trust takes time. Working slowly, respectfully, gently, and with complete presence, over time is the fastest way to resolve issues with parts.

SELF-leadership, for me, is compassionately seeing and caring for all of my parts, building connection and trust, so that SELF may benevolently lead. My goal is not to coach, teach, or parent my parts. It isn't even about healing or overcoming, even though often that happens. For example, if I am feeling afraid, my goal is no longer to eliminate or "get over" my fears, but to lead and care for my Fearful Parts from SELF-energy. The natural result of this SELF-leadership is confidence and courage.

calm
connected
compassionate
curious
confident
creative
clear
courageous

Finally, while there is no specific order to the 8Cs and, I noticed, for my unique system, this order is very helpful to me — each energy begets the next energy. To have Courage, Clarity, Creativity, and Confidence, I have to begin with Calm, Connected, Compassion, and Curiosity! For me it's the perfect life and business plan!

# Rebel Against the Bullshit of Conditioned Disconnection and Rejection

Our harsh, inward self-criticism and judgment are so deeply ingrained. In myself and in my clients, I notice a silent sentence stem at the end of many of our thoughts which maintains the disconnection and self rejection. That need for attachment — that Dr. Maté showed me — overrides and conditions us to incessantly be judging and rejecting ourselves in a perpetual state of disconnection.

I can't stand it a moment longer.

The silent disconnection hurts and hurts and hurts, and the hurts pile up and live in our bodies and show up in our being. I want to be present, connected to myself, without having to have perfect thoughts or circumstances. I want to be more loving and accepting of all of my parts. I want to rebel against the bullshit I was conditioned to believe, and I am inviting you to do the same. I've got a new practice for us to begin nurturing and reconditioning our Self-Connection.

Here's what it looks like in real time:

It's been a while since I've spent time in my book. *And, I'm doing it wrong.*

I've had to care for sick dogs and sick kids and a sick dad. *And I'm behind.*

I'm scattered this morning and didn't get everything in order for sacred writing time today. *And, I'm failing and wrong.*

I didn't sleep well and I'm not feeling great, and tears are at the surface. *And I'm a horrible person.*

The italics are the silent disconnecting thoughts that sneak in uninvited.

Here, I began to notice the disconnection and I was able to drop in slightly, reconnect physically, mentally, emotionally, and realize it's all OK.

Lots of distractions and that's OK.

Dogs barking next door and that's OK.

I feel delayed on my book writing and I love me.

I make up stories about all I should be accomplishing and I love me.

I can only do so much, and I DO do so much and I LOVE ME.

There are things at the front of my head and on the sides that take away my attention and I LOVE ME.

I've been spending TONS of money lately and I LOVE ME.

I can always make more money and I LOVE ME.

Deep breath in and I LOVE ME.

Writing and typing feels good and I LOVE ME.

Perhaps write about and I LOVE ME . . . We all need more "And, I LOVE ME" at the end of our thoughts.

My body started out scattered and dense, but slowly I slipped into a bit of neutral acceptance with "what is" when my afterthought became, "and it's ok." Then I remembered the practice I share with my clients, "And I LOVE ME!" The thoughts in my head became lighter instantly, and my body began to feel energized just by removing the making of myself wrong, and by reminding myself that no matter what I feel, I LOVE ME.

This silently making ourselves wrong is subconsciously — or maybe even for some, consciously — running around our inner worlds leaving a heavy, wet, blanket and stealing our connection to Self. Some call this inner judge the Inner Critic. My inner parts that make me wrong just use that as a tool to beg me for connection. And when I practice, And I LOVE ME, they feel my connection and begin to relax.

My Gawd. Its a fucking miracle to stop rejecting all parts of you and start welcoming all parts with presence and connection. Five stars. Ten out of ten. Highly recommended.

# Being Misunderstood

What if people don't understand me? What if they see everything I say and do wrong?

A business owner client with twenty-five years of success in multiple lanes asked me those questions in a session. Ugh. In my chest and the back of my throat, I actually felt the pain alongside her. It's human to want to be known and to be understood, and for some of us, this is an old and deep pain that has been buried, and buried for a lifetime.

Many highly successful people know that we are stable and safe — we intellectually know that we are able to work on healing, processing emotions, and releasing behaviors that helped us survive yet no longer serve us. Many of us also have spent a lifetime bending who we are to fit the systems, the structures, the expectations of others. We've spent a lifetime getting to know the person we *think* we should be.

Perhaps, for some of us, it hurts so much to be misunderstood because we so deeply misunderstand ourselves.

When this cluster of parts gets activated in me, and they recently did, parts of me felt accused, defensive, and deeply afraid that I was "doing it wrong." These parts have been so accustomed to performing for others that they weren't able to trust our own knowing. I'm still building trust with them, that I won't leave them, I won't abandon them, and I won't withdraw my love and connection from them. Only when SELF came in and understood these parts via presence and curiosity, when SELF helps witness their fears and concerns, are they able to see the "we've done nothing wrong" and stand in calm, clear response when the accusations are made. Neutral, compassionate, and frankly, take-no-shit clarity.

There are so many unexplored and unwitnessed parts of ourselves. It can be terrifying to "meet" or "know" these parts, until it becomes the work we "can't NOT do."

I am committed to getting to know all parts of me, especially the parts I misunderstand, or the parts who have been exiled away. I'm committed to understanding my benevolent and fierce protectors. I can see that they are tired, and perhaps if I got to know them better, they would rest. And then — when someone else misunderstands me — it won't hurt so bad.

# Don't Lose Your Music

I'm pretty sure I was conceived somewhere in the Hill Country with Willie Nelson's music in the background. As a Gen X woman, I love me some '80s rock and pop, but the music of my soul has always been country. My Gawd, I danced my blue jeans and boots' ass through college in Honky Tonks at the end of county roads. (I know, earlier, I said I don't like dancing, but there was this one season of exception in the nineties).

When I got married for the first time, that man loved screaming, heavy metal, bang-bang-noise music. He used to carry his drumsticks in the car and bang along to the intense anger thumping out of his speakers. He hated country music. I hated his heavy, angry music.

When we rode together in the car, as married couples do, we settled on Mix 94.7 — a local Austin station that still exists, and that plays a mix of mainstream "modern adult contemporary and modern pop" music. Even when I rode in my own car alone, my radio remained fixed on that station. The dial stayed on "good enough" instead of tuning back to my soul.

After my divorce, and long after he and I stopped sharing car rides, I hopped into my truck one day, turned on the engine, and out of the speakers came that mainstream pop. Then and there I was hit with the realization that I'd lost my music! I had given it up for him, and even after he left, I had forgotten to give it back to myself. I promptly reset the preset stations accordingly.

Compromise in shared spaces is fine. Just don't lose your own gawd-damned music.

# How to Be You: A Primer for the Uninitiated

To be you,
You have to trust you.
To trust you,
You have to actually KNOW you.
To know you,
You must be willing to meet
And connect to *all* of you.

ALL of you.

# The Vulnerability
# of Criticism and Conflict

I've got a little secret. Well, it's not so much a secret as it is just something I don't talk about all the time. No matter how confident I am, an unanticipated harsh or uninformed critique or contrary opinion can unravel all my armor and razor-slice the heart of the little one inside me.

Part of me is ashamed that I seek so much agreement.

All these outer layers — essentially my armor — know what to say, they understand projection, and they can receive warranted or respected feedback, but take one step over the line of my adulthood and you will hit my deepest and trembling inner wounds.

The Instagram therapy memes have me understanding that I might have developed some attachment stuff growing up. Parts of me can be so sensitive to conflict and criticism. In these moments, even though I logically know the conflict or criticism isn't personal, my protectors are relentless about their job of making sure I don't get hurt that way again.

I've learned to slow way down in these moments, mostly. My once unregulated and Unfiltered Rage that would erupt when I was afraid has now been discovered for who she really is. It wasn't until five years into my second marriage, and in my early forties, that I met and understood this part of me. One day in a fight with my husband, I felt the heat of the rage rise up in my body, my armpits sweating and my jaw crushing my teeth together and my eyes narrowing with heat. And, instead of engaging in round after round of our typical arguments, I paused.

I read a marriage book once that said, when you feel the familiar pull of "the same old fight" with your partner, STOP.

Stop. That made sense. And, for the first time, in this fight with Bill, I did. I paused my rage and told my husband I needed a time-out. I slowly backed into the bathroom and sat on the tub, and I just listened within. There, alongside my slowing breath, I heard her — the little one inside who said, "I'm terrified . . . just so afraid he'll leave. All men leave."

The rage, the wars I perpetuated, were simply a front for the vulnerability and tenderness I felt. That little one and her protectors were not forty-something, they were very young, and scared. I just sat there with this little frightened one for a moment. Breathing together. Being together. Me and my terrified tender part who was so scared of being left. I let her know I would never leave her.

There on the edge of the bathtub, I was able to connect and care for this part of me, and she began to relax.

After I came out of the bathroom, my energy and demeanor shifted, I told my husband that I wasn't angry. I apologized for my vitriol and loud words and I confessed that I was just deeply scared. At that moment both our shoulders dropped and all the weapons that we used to defend ourselves were released.

"I will never leave you, you are my wife," he said, genuinely, as if it was absurd for me to consider he would go like the others in my life had, over and over.

The little one inside is a lousy interpreter of meaning. She seems to automatically think that any displeased person, any disagreement, or any perceived criticism = danger, and so she hides, while my raging protectors fight.

These days, I am the full-body noticer of all of this. And as I notice these parts have their squabbles, I am most often able to just be there, in the center, grounding and calming these parts down — not with some wise words, or by obliterating them into the shadows again, but by simply *being there* with them in full presence, open heart, curious intent.

>Presence.
>Listening.
>Hearing.
>Grounding.
>Meeting.

>And being with all of me.

# No Really, All Parts Welcome

"You're doing the exercise wrong, this is inappropriate."

As soon as my coaching partner said the words, I felt the familiar tightness seize my chest and the tears in my sinuses start to well up. I sat perfectly still, trying to hold the impending flooding back, thankful that my glasses might hide my watering eyes, at least for a bit.

My brain started condemning me with shame for being so sensitive, for trusting, for getting it wrong, for screwing up in front of an important teacher in a field I loved. My jaw tightened and I felt my hands roll into fists — my defensive and aggressive parts were beginning to surface.

A hundred threatened parts, all locked and loaded. With a quivering lip, I breathed deeply until the call ended, and then I let them all loose and sobbed while all the thinking parts in my head shared their strong protective and critical opinions. The loudest was Shame.

> "How on Earth can I be this reactive and sensitive to a jackass like that?"

> "You are fucked up and should be locked away — not out there leading and coaching."

> "You need to withdraw from any public life because it is not safe to interact with anyone if this bullshit can get unlocked so easily."

> "You are irretrievably broken — this is your kryptonite."

These instantaneous hypersensitive episodes happen to me about three times a year. They always come on without any warning, no intuition, and always after seemingly small, disproportionate triggers. Something deep in me sneaks to the surface and perceives a substantial and unfounded withdrawal of approval, love, or respect.

These episodes leave me utterly mortified, and it's an entire fucking "parts-led party" in my head for two or three days after each incident. My thinking parts are trying to reconcile some logic and formula that will make it all make sense, so it will never happen again.

Each time this occurs, something else in me so generously reminds me of each and every time this has happened to me in the past, and then I relive the moment of impact of the worst of those events. One moment becomes all the moments like this. It is a physical and emotional gut punch that knocks the wind out of me, at times, for days, and on the worst occasions, weeks.

I have learned that this is a symptom that almost 100 percent of people with ADHD experience: Rejection Sensitive Dysphoria.[10] It's not a diagnosis, but a collection of symptoms. This label helps, and it doesn't. The research shows that it is neurologic and genetic. That helps, and it doesn't.

Yay, I'm not alone. Not yay, can this be overcome and healed? Am I stuck with this affliction forever? Is another landmine around the next corner?

With compassionate parts work, I am finding relief for it and it doesn't live so long in my head or thoughts. I am more skilled at providing relief for others than I am for myself, but I am learning to reach out for the specific help *I* need when my system is in acute distress, so that I can simply be somatically present with all these parts.

Presence. Calm presence. One slow and gentle breath — with awareness — at a time. No fixing, no coaching, no teaching, no bypassing, just in the same room of my being — all together. Even the Shame. These extreme parts of me both want to be seen and felt, and sometimes heard. The path to healing is the one that feels the most dangerous. Sit in the room and breathe the same air as these parts. Give them space.

Parts of me squirm, like a nervous tic. I do my best to notice each sensation. I pay attention to my thoughts without believing them, giving them compassionate energy, not another argument or reprimand.

In IFS, when we say, "All Parts Welcome," this is the work. Not just the easy parts, the mild parts, but *these* parts. I'm not there yet. I'm still learning the full-body skills of leading myself, from SELF, and again I am reminded that just because we know it in our minds doesn't mean we BE it in our whole being.

This is the work. It's a *deeeeep* inside, whole body and whole being job.

It's the work I came to do. I came to swing wide, to be a woman of range, and to navigate the edges of being human. I asked Gawd to help me have an open heart, and she is introducing me to my body and all her wisdom. She is teaching me, moment by moment — with each unexpected trigger and emotional meltdown — that I am complete love, no matter what. ALL OF ME. She is teaching me to connect with and care for ALL OF ME.

# There, There

. . . there, there . . . FEAR,
I see you.
I will not leave you.
I am here for you.

# A Reminder to Breathe

Breathe Y'all.

Perfect is not better. Polished is not better. Simply showing up is often more than enough.

The reason I share my stories and so much of my personal life is because I have realized that I am the other you. You are not alone. I am not alone. My personal stories may be dressed in a different outfit, but underneath that shell our stories are the same. The essence and the energy are the same.

What is that project in which you're not willing to let yourself be a beginner?

Where are you making yourself be perfect? This is your little love nudge to remind you to get back up after a fall, get back to aligned work, take one small step forward, keep going, and be persistent. Rest when you need to, but keep doing the work. Let it be what it is. Perfection is the death of creation, and you aren't here to be perfect — you're here to create.

Breathe, Babe, reconnect with you, your head, your heart, your body, and all your parts.

Presence. Connection. Compassion. Breath. These things produce clarity, creativity, courage, and confidence.

This is my business plan. This is my life plan. This is my spiritual plan. Get in alignment and then . . . Breathe in and listen. When I do this I open myself to hear the wisdom: breathe, babe, everything is working.

You working harder and faster and chasing perfection won't make anything easier or better.

Breathe, babe. Get back to reading books. Reconnect with the word and stories and inspiration on the page.

Breathe, babe. Everything can change in a moment.

You are the decider. You are the maker of change and action. You are also a being capable of surrender, and you *know* that control is an illusion. This is the paradox. Being willing to live in the paradox, being willing to contradict ourselves, being willing to live in the middle of the both/and, we realize our potential and the possibility in front of us in this moment. I am both responsible to take action to choose my attitude AND to choose my actions to make a move. I am in control of absolutely nothing. I surrender with each breath and ask Spirit for help and guidance, trusting in all my actions and knowing that if everything goes to shit, I'm still held.

Breathe, babe.

What does your Spirit say to you when you slow down and breathe? Right here and now. Listen in between the breaths. Listen to the wisdom that comes up from inside of you.

Breathe, babe.

Allow that breath to drop below your shoulders, your clavicle, your ribs, your chest, all the way down into your belly, to your hips. Allow it to go slow: in through your nose, and out through your nose. Allow your belly to fill, not just your chest. Breathe all the way down to your toes and listen. Exhale even longer than your inhale and listen.

Here's what I hear: Everything is working perfectly. You can't fuck this up. You've got this. Everything can change on a dime. And not just for the "worst," by the way. Sure. Our brain is trained to see that everything can change on a dime for the worst instead of, everything can change for the better.

Settle in. Create peace. Create connection. Create presence with all of you. Create all the things you value on a daily basis, no more excuses. It's time to get back to the business of being, of being, of being. Three times more being than the doing, because the BE is more important than the DO, and it must come first.

What do you have to believe about who you BE? Reconnect with your whole SELF and breathe.

> *"What you are looking for is already in you . . .*
> *You already are everything you are seeking."*
> *~Thich Nhat Hanh*

Thank you, Thich Nhat Hanh.

Breathe, babe.

Take this moment, and listen to the wisdom that already lives inside of you. Notice different distinctions you hear in your brain, in your thinking, in your body, in your being. And if any of this is confusing for you, you are not alone. If you are wondering how to surrender, if you are thinking that when you are quiet you don't hear anything, it's all perfect. There, there Silence, I see you. I won't leave you.

Breathe, babe, slow down.

Slow smooths things out and ultimately speeds things up. But how do I slow down with all this stuff on my to do list?

I can tell you all day long that slowing down, breathing, and listening is actually the best way to get your to-do list done. But you won't believe me until you begin to experiment with it for yourself. Be willing to experiment. Everything does not need to be so fucking perfect. Let it be playful. Let it be messy. Let it be imperfect and uncertain. Let it be an experiment. Test it out. Give it a go.

What if everything works out?

# HOW

HOW, how, how?

These are the types of questions I hear over and over. Most of the time How isn't a very useful question. *How* questions actually stop the brain from creating and envisioning. It's a question that we ask from a state of disempowerment. It can point to our need for certainty and perfection. If we always need it to be perfect, our work will never see the light of day. It will remain a gem in our minds and no one will ever know its brilliance.

If you want to increase your personal power, start asking WHAT questions. What can I do next? What would help? What would I like to feel? What would the next tiny step be? Or WHO questions: Who could help me with this? Who do I know? Those two types of questions: WHAT and WHO will empower you.

If you are still stuck on the HOW question, step one is Google it. Ask Siri. Yep. I said it. Google that shit. I'm kind of a smartass that way. And it's actually really true. You can find the HOW for most things with some simple research.

Strategically, step one is simple: Google it. Underneath the tactical outer strategy — what really is helpful is to let there be a "full being" pre-strategy. What's this you ask? The real HOW to is always stop and breathe. In an argument with your spouse? Stop, breathe. Frustrated with technology? Stop, breathe. Want to know how to fill your roster? Stop, breathe. Want to know how to make a million bucks? Stop, breathe. Want to know how to heal your body? Stop and breathe.

I don't know what questions you're asking right now. I'll bet when you slow down, breathe, and listen deeply, you will find your answer. Listen in the space of your breath. The answers are right there, waiting for you. The wisdom to keep going forward is right there. The way to organize your brain is right there.

The piece that you're seeking is seeking you.

The prosperity you're seeking is seeking you. Be like my sweet boxer, Leroy Brown, who often plants himself six feet away from me on the floor. Take one of those big settling in dog breaths that lets your whole body melt.

Just breathe.

# What Heather Says

"Mind slowing down, Body slowing down." My book publisher and coach[11] always says this to me when we begin to share space writing. If that isn't the best damn life advice right there. Life rushes us. Scurry, scurry. Stay numb, move fast, do more, more, more. This is the whisper of the invisible systems.

Slowing down gives us presence, and in presence, we can connect to Sacred SELF.

So that's what I am doing at this very moment as I write these words. I am taking the space that I need. I sit here at my beloved wood desk from Pottery Barn circa 1997 allowing myself to soak in the joys and delights of my life that surround me here.

To my right, are my nine journals — some for classes, some for work, some for life, some for painting, some for business planning, all for joy. Everywhere I look I see the colors of my life on homemade posters, my whiteboard, 2x3 and 5x7 notecards on my desk.

My box of favorite pink lip glosses, the books I'm devouring right now. Photos of my dogs, the artwork I've created and had framed. The smell of incense (Nag champa) over my right shoulder is beginning to gently fill the room.

On my left, my thirty-ounce, yellow, stainless steel cup with cool drinking water and a collection of watercolor paint brushes. A turquoise art cart with way more paints than I can ever use, even though I paint almost every day. A ring light — this ensures that I look as cute and bright as I feel on the video calls I do a few times a week with clients, colleagues, and friends. And on the floor at the door of my office is my big white twelve-year-old rescued boxer, Leroy Brown. Closer to my chair (I notice they are unusually in their opposite "spots"), Clementine, my nine-year-old rescue boxer rests "frog-dog-style" with her cute little bootie and nubby tail facing me.

The magnetic whiteboard in front of me, rainbow-colored lists of the values and essences I'm cultivating in my life. More posters — visual models of the human behavior, emotion, thinking, and parts-work I do with myself and with my clients. Color swatches from various paint palettes are held with pink plastic magnets to the wall. A small painting of an outstretched arm in a striped, black and white shirt, offering a bouquet of snapdragons and wildflowers, wrapped in light brown parchment paper.

And then there is a photo of my large family back when there were only nineteen of us. I see the faces of my mom and dad, my two brothers, two sisters, their families, two of my cousins, and these amazing miracles that are my nieces and nephews, our future, all Crows. The lighting in the photo is bad, and since then, baby Bowman has been born and just recently, baby Rayne was born into our family as well. The joyful love I have for my family gets stuck in my throat for a moment.

At my feet, I feel the indulgence and softness of the ergonomic footstool that I gifted to myself. My back and hips are held by the "big man" chair I invested in last season. It's creaking and may need some lubrication at the joints. In my ears, calming music from one of my favorite playlists comes across the invisible interweb wires.

I get to be here, in this moment. I breathe in the anticipation of this moment eventually weaving through time, being printed on a page and bound in a book, inviting you to do what Heather invites us to do:

"Mind Slowing Down, Body Slowing Down."

# SELF-Centered

I've come to have a philosophy about being SELF-centered. Of course, many of us grew up being told not to be selfish, to NOT be "so self-centered." I wasn't taught that there was a way to care for myself that also didn't make me a selfish jerk, and so like many others, I grew up to be an over-functioning, over-giving, people pleaser. Over-functioning in that I subconsciously took responsibility for others' emotions more than mine, and a people pleaser in that it became my way of being, to bend and twist myself in order to be liked. Until I really examined this way of being, I thought I was being kind and nice. What I was really being, was a fearful manipulator — manipulating people with contrived behavior and manners because I was so subconsciously afraid of losing connection.

My orbit danced around others out of fear of being rejected, and it left me in a world of wonky relationships. I especially did this with boyfriends in my youth and young adulthood, and as a grown woman, I did it in business and with friends. The consequence of orbiting around others was sacrificing anything that was my own — my own desires, my ability to receive, feeling taken for granted, and storing up resentment because I gave so much of myself away.

Being raised in a school that taught me to do the dance of goodness for my salvation, and taking on the good girl persona in order to avoid losing my deepest inner longing for connection and belonging, left nothing of ME. How could I BE myself, if I didn't know myself? I certainly couldn't trust a ME I really didn't know. I was in my forties when I really began my journey into what being me really meant, and I began to shift the meaning of the phrase self-centered to SELF-centered.

My hypothesis? If I could be truly SELF-centered, centered in SELF, filled from within with the love for me that I craved so desperately, then I would actually be the best me for others as well. Being SELF-centered was actually the most considerate way of being as we move through this life. If I were SELF-centered, not only would I be my best self from the inside, but anyone who came into my orbit would receive the best of me — the authentic and SELF-led me. How could that *not* be the most loving thing I could give my life and the communities around me? Naturally, some people would be disappointed and find me unpleasant — rejection would be inevitable either way, but I wouldn't be rejecting ME.

THIS I can work with. This is the nourishment that I want you to have, should you choose it.

> I will never abandon myself.
> I will never ghost myself.
> I will always be here for me.
> I will always love myself.
> I will trust myself.
> I will affirm and adore myself.
> I will care for myself.
> I will validate myself.
> I will see and hear myself, wholly.

I am here for all parts of me and this welcoming — this befriending — is everything.

# SELF-Connected

As a protective coping mechanism, I lived much of my life disconnected and disassociated. I could see all the ways I would leave my own body and being when I felt threatened, especially emotionally.

After acknowledging my willingness to be SELF-centered came my awareness of SELF-connection, or actually, my lack of SELF-connection. I began to see that so much of my energy was up in my head with my thinking parts. When I get scared, I go to my head — trying to intellectually solve problems by grasping for certainty. My thinking parts have been so helpful all my life, but there is a deeper connection calling me. I've spoken about learning to be more in my body and slowing down in other sections of this work. Here, I want to share how my thinking parts and disconnected parts have updated and made way for the energy of mySELF. They now work together through SELF-connection.

SELF-connection and SELF-leadership are verbal anchors that represent the way I BE with all of my parts. Instead of letting the protective parts of me react and run the show of my life, slowing down and tapping in has helped me build trusting relationships with these parts from my most sacred CORE SELF.

> "Becoming a leader is synonymous with becoming yourself. It is precisely that simple and also that difficult."
>
> — Deidra Towns[12]

For many years I was grasping in this direction — looking to the Divine in me as my center and my achievements as proof of success. I now realize my motive was achievement-based instead of relationship-based. Then, my drive propelled me to completely evolve past my fears, anxieties, and core wounds, to overcome them once and for all. Now I can see how I spent most of a lifetime trying to escape my humanity. My sweet, holy, humanity. Only when I was introduced to the IFS framework did this sacred internal order click into possibility and place for me.

Instead of overcoming and banishing fears (a truly impossible task), I could learn how to *lead* my fears. I could get to know them, understand them, witness them, and hold them with compassion and care.

The long fuzzy blond-haired second-grader in me was delighted and relieved as I found this work. She knew the importance of relationships and connection even then. She begged the towering-old-man-scary Minister of Youth at the evangelical school to allow her to lead the prayer in morning chapel, specifically to assure her fellow elementary students that damnation was not the most loving focus, contrary to what we were being continually told — but that *relationships and connection* with God, ourselves, and others were . . . She soaked all of this in!

I can see her in my mind's eye, wearing a plaid pinafore dress and crisp white short-sleeve shirt — plopping back into the softness of a giant cozy sofa chair, a relieved smile on her face! "Finally, and now I can rest."

Thank you little Allison, for always pointing me to CONNECTION.

I share myself and my voice so that you may — should you choose — remember how powerful you are. I share so that we may both remember we are the love and acceptance we seek. I speak in first-person to own my experience. As you read this, it can be about me. And, it is also available to be about you.

- ♡ SELF
- ♡ SELF-connection
- ♡ SELF-presence
- ♡ SELF-love
- ♡ SELF-leadership
- ♡ SELF-creation
- ♡ SELF-identity
- ♡ SELF-belief
- ♡ SELF-being
- ♡ SELF-expression

- ♡ SELF-experience
- ♡ SELF-wealth
- ♡ SELF-joy
- ♡ SELF-validation
- ♡ SELF-acknowledgement
- ♡ SELF-advocacy
- ♡ SELF-freedom
- ♡ SELF-peace
- ♡ SELF-calm
- ♡ SELF-compassion

The relationship I have with mySELF is the generation of all my being. From this place, I experience everything and everyone.

What would it be like to move about the world with more of an open heart, for myself and for others? Sometimes I create an experience of misery, tension, and unhappiness through my judgment of myself, through rejecting myself. I recognize this, and then am able to meet the judgment and rejection with my compassionate presence. In these instances, contentment begins to return. No change in physical circumstance — just meeting and welcoming the part of me that has such harsh self-judgment, meeting the parts of me that are so afraid.

What does this bring? Freedom.

To open my heart, I must compassionately and curiously welcome the parts of me that are afraid, angry, untrusting, defensive, and closed. Not reject or bypass them (which I spent a lifetime doing, to no avail). These parts are activated often, and instead of shaming them away, I am learning to move toward them. It is a practice, a way of being with myself, and slowly becoming a new normal. In the past, I escaped these moments by being unconsciously reactive. Sometimes I find my escaping parts still leading. I am learning. I am practicing.

I am welcoming all parts of myself, especially my most uncomfortable, unacceptable parts:

- My fearful parts

- My "judgy" parts

- The parts of me that boil with hate

- My parts that grasp for certainty

- The parts of me that need to feel above others intellectually

- My parts that are terrified of being rejected and left

- My grudge-holding parts

- The parts that want to cuss people out on Twitter

- The parts that want to punch people in the face

- My over-functioning parts

- My under-functioning parts

- My sadness, loss, and grief parts

- My hyper-independent parts

- The parts of me that boil with hate

- The parts that crave validation and attention

- My disconnected and disassociating parts

- My ashamed to stand tall parts

- My mean parts

- My depression and my anxiety parts

- My coachy parts

- My need-to-fix-it-all parts

- My need-to-KNOW -and-UNDERSTAND brainy parts

- Did I mention my judging parts?

And so many more. I am befriending these parts instead of rejecting them. I embrace . . .

PRESENCE
CALM
CONNECTED
COMPASSIONATE
CURIOUS
CONFIDENT
CREATIVE
CLEAR
COURAGEOUS

As Buddha reminds me, I, more than anyone, deserve my own love and affection, my own acknowledgement. Opening my own heart to all parts of myself helps me open my heart to the world. You, more than anyone, deserve your own love and affection, too. I choose to spend intentional time doing this, being this. Sorting through and spending time relating with my parts, and mySELF. These SELF practices are the fulcrum, the power, the most effective things I do.

When I say effective, I mean better relationships, stronger boundaries, more inner peace, and yes, more of the great almighty dollar. My vision map and goal list are less about accomplishment or acquisition and more about deepening my commitment to nourishing mind, body, spirit, and inner system practices. My state of being puts SELF-energy at the helm to lead and guide all parts of me.

Through meeting and moving toward myself, I build self-trust. In knowing all my parts and in trusting mySELF, I am able to remember who I AM, and I AM able to easily BE more ME. This is my purpose for existing. I share openly as a gift to perhaps inspire YOU to RememBEr who you BE. Your BEING is *your* creation. I choose practice and intention versus leaving it to chance.

# A New Relationship

I wish BEING YOURSELF was as easy as flipping a switch. Heck, I wish it was as easy as saying or making a simple decision. The truth is, we don't *know* ourselves completely. We are taught from birth to annihilate, suppress, reject, and exile parts of ourselves. We are taught to judge and shame and bypass and hide and mask parts of ourselves.

As I talk with clients these days, I hear them lament the "dark spots" within themselves — parts they shove away and try to escape. And they are exhausted — their parts are exhausted. Pathologizing and ignoring only makes the "dark spots" bigger.

You know this. I know this. So what do we actually do? Just like we learned shame and judgment, we can learn to meet and BE with all of our parts. Not to coach them, or fix them, or even send them to the light.

Seriously. Fuck off with your positivity and light at all costs shit. It's violent and harmful. And If I ever did it to you, I'm deeply sorry. Learning to meet and BE present, connected, and compassionate with our most hidden parts is — frankly — a new relationship.

You can't have wholeness while simultaneously dismissing some of the parts. But, you've been taught to fear them. What if they have wisdom for you? What if you actually knew how to BE with your grief, or sadness, or rage, or shame, or your too-much parts, or your not-enough parts?

Get to know all of your parts. Through presence, connection, and curiosity, get to know your internal family. Get to actually know yourself.

# PART 3

Calm

# Hey, Head-Led
# People Like Me!

Calm isn't just an idea — it is a physical state of a regulated nervous system. I used to fiercely believe that my state of BEING was primary, and that from this place I could create anything in life. There is a foundation even more primary — one that positions us for our state of BEING — and that, my friends, is the calm and regulated nervous system.

Until recently, I only ever had a mostly intellectual awareness about my nervous system. And as evidenced by the at least forty-one other mentions of "nervous system" in this book, it has become, with both grief, and relief, foundational.

Grief because I remember being taught about the nervous system in junior high. I also remember a brief lesson in high school biology. These lessons were a blip. In all my undergraduate and graduate and postgraduate studies — in all my coaching training — the nervous system was never more than a blip, but I now see being able to regulate and calm our nervous systems is foundational.

I grieve the effort I put into my mind, understanding, and mindset, when all along the restoration, peace, and healing I craved was a somatic thing, a practice thing, a body thing. For someone like me who grew up in a home of dysregulated beings, how could I possibly understand in my body how very foundational the regulation and calming of the nervous system is.

Relief because if we keep searching we eventually get what we need — and I'm trusting — at the right time. At the beginning of this book, I posed the question to myself, "Who would I have to

BE, to be the woman who writes this book?" When I first began writing, I believed I would need to have an emotional or mental shift to write this book. While this is true and remains part of the answer, the other part is something even deeper. To write this book, I had to BE presence and calm in my body. I had to become aware of the profound impact a jacked nervous system would have on, well, *everything*.

Our most recent foster dog, a traumatized and injured Boston terrier, Harry B. Styles, whom I impulsively agreed to foster one morning when I was emotionally grasping for something to control, and something to appreciate me, was the reason this lesson landed. I have fostered a dozen puppies over the years. I know all the dog trainy things. And when we brought Harry home, the normal integration into our lives did not go well.

Harry had been dumped on a shelter doorstep in the middle of the night with a severely injured eyeball. It was hanging out of its socket. He was left by his people and badly hurt, only to have emergency surgery and then recover in a shelter vet hospital with many other scared and loud dogs.

I wish that calm could be created with one hug, a safe home, a soft bed, and love. Calm takes time, though. It takes slow. It takes little to no extra stimulation. And I tried to bring this sweet baby into my home with my two older and somewhat anxious dogs. Our normal separation and meet-and-greet time was not nearly enough. The high-pitched barking between all three dogs, even when they were separated, pierced into my chest, and resulted in increasing my anxiety and sadness. The irritation for the first week in our home was relentless. I let the rescue organization know I might have made a mistake, and that perhaps we weren't the best foster home for this dog. The safety of all three dogs and my sanity was at stake.

The rescue gal put me in touch with their trainer, and we had a good, long call about the dogs. In my frantic state, I assured him I *knew* all the things, but they weren't working . . . blah . . . blah . . .

blah . . . and he assured me that this dog was not a problem. The dog trainer insisted that Harry just needed two to three weeks of decompression. Saving you all the details, the trainer gave me a set of instructions for a training technique called a "Behavioral Down"[13] and, while still on the phone with me he had me look for a particular visual in his paperwork.

It was a chart called "Reactive vs. Cognitive."[14] I had heard the term reactive many times before when training my dogs. I knew about taking care not to reinforce reactive behavior. I knew about positively rewarding good behavior. But what this man said to me as I looked at that image was pivotal: "Your dog's brain can't learn anything while it's in a reactive state. He can only learn new behaviors when he is calm."

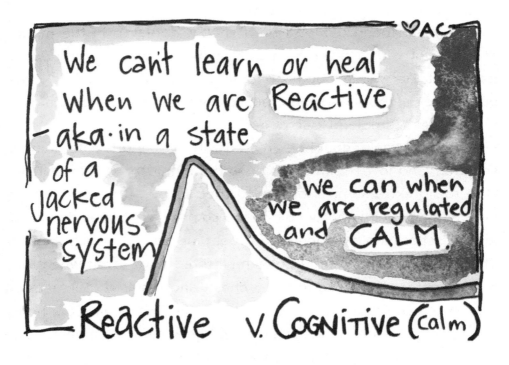

In that moment, all the bits and blips I've learned over the years landed in my deepest understanding. Perhaps it was my own fried and frantic nervous system in that moment that made me see that no intellectual KNOWING alone could shift things. Only getting myself, and my dogs, to calm.

How could I have been a performance and behavior coach for eighteen years and not understand how much nervous system dysregulation impacts performance and behavior? UGH. I will never forget again, because I finally *felt* it, instead of just thinking it. By opening my body to the sensations of all that I am, all that I have learned, and all that I have felt in the classroom and in my life, I am *finally* becoming a woman who *knows* instead of knows.

You and I, our heads and smarts have created so much in our lives. We care for people, we solve problems in our heads continually. Understanding gives us relief but not quite enough for lasting change or peace. Maybe this is what the meditators were always trying to tell me, but sitting still has always been hard for me, and even harder, is slowing my thinking down. Attempting to meditate from my almost always reactive state (even when I appeared calm) like so many of my perfectly capable peers were able to do, only triggered more reactivity.

Thinking and understanding as strengths can be a sneaky way for many of us to escape the difficult feelings and emotions of our bodies. If you feel the disconnect between all your wisdom and knowing, and the glitch of your lived experience, I invite you to consider your body and nervous system. Gently, slowly, compassionately (and perhaps with trauma-informed care), somatic and sensory work to begin to learn to BE IN YOUR BODY.

Breath and Slow Tango were my gateway drugs. Walking in nature and earthing are helping me pay attention to the visceral sensations in my body and to make connections between my intellectual thinking experience of emotions and the actual physicality of those feelings. And, I've just started experimenting with a practice called Havening[15]. Practice is the key word for all these things. Just like the "Behavioral Down" training method teaches my dogs, I can use methods to SELF-calm, but everything takes practice, time, and repetition.

My nervous system calming practices have become the highest priority in my life. I can see clearly now, that everything I desire is on the other side of, and created through, a calm and regulated nervous system.

# Judgment Destroys Calm

"What if you didn't judge it . . . that circumstance, that already-miserable thing that happened; what if you didn't judge it?" As Pema Chödrön says regarding when things fall apart:

> "Just feel the rage, feel the shame, feel the guilt, feel the remorse, feel the resentment, feel the heat - feel the fire - just as it is. Just as it is. Just as it is - not escalating further, not repressing, not turning it into something hard..."
>
> - Pema Chödrön[16]

We thinking humans often make things so much harder than they already are by judging. What if you didn't judge it?

# Capacity

I was an early February baby, my sweet mom's first. For her and me, a magical kind of love was born that day. Over the years, hearts began to permeate my life: heart-shaped cakes, heart-shaped boxes, heart jewelry and hearts on my clothes and journals. Even today, a hand-drawn yellow heart is in my professional brand. It shifted from red to yellow to remind me of the Spirit inside of me.

I don't remember ever not having an awareness of hearts, both in form and in my emotional and physical body. I also have distinct memories of thoughts and feelings that seemed to come from deep within me. In my little-girl being was a vast liberty . . . before she even knew what that word meant.

There are so many moments in my heart and mind lately. They pop in and out of my awareness and I see all the little seasons of life lived in my forty-nine years. With a few breaths as I write, I can viscerally tap in, and these memories come to mind:

> I would feel the physical sensation of warmth and love around animals — dogs, cats, squirrels, and especially horses. Occasionally, I would find myself in the presence of horses, and my heart felt two sizes bigger. I could bring this feeling to me as I played alone in my room with my model horses and dolls under my big yellow corner dresser. I felt pure delight in creating relationships with these beings.
>
> I have a sense of a memory of being out in nature in a field of taller grasses and a big open sky. As I sink into

that memory, I have a deep feeling of unguardedness and wholeness.

Finally, the lightness of being I felt in the water — especially in a pool (because I was afraid of the fish in the lakes). Swimming felt like the safest and softest place to be. My body wasn't bound by gravity in the water. The crystal clear and clean water, caressing my skin and holding my floating body, regulated my nervous system.

There are no other people in these free and open-hearted moments and memories. When I tap in to remember myself in the presence of people, I can feel my guard go up and a constriction in my being. I felt more connected and safe in the presence of a twelve-hundred-pound horse than in the presence of humans I knew and loved. I craved people, relationships, and connection, but they were not my safe haven.

(Mom, I know you are reading this. I'm sorry if these words hurt. You and Dad did good. I know you love me. I knew it then. I don't think any of us felt safe in our bodies, including you and Dad.)

I now know that somewhere in the melting pot of nature + nurture + lived experience, we begin to pick up our armor over time. Our foundational needs — physiological, safety, love and belonging, esteem — these get bumped and bruised, so we naturally develop these protective coping behaviors. My experience of this led me to a closed and defended heart, hidden under the armor of delusional optimism.

Nature + nurture + lived experience + choice helped me decide to do something different. I decided to take on the journey of an unarmored heart and be a transparent leader along the way. Self-discovery is the greatest adventure I've ever been on. And somehow, life turned me clearly toward a career — a dharma — of soul work helping people do the same.

I know the pain of the positivity bypass, the shame of my inner experience being vastly different from what the world sees. I know the isolation and loneliness of guarding my heart so doggedly. The armor is heavy. Protection is a helpful tool when used wisely and in service of the moment. However, carrying the protection all the time dims our capacity for fully living. As we meet our whole selves, even and especially the darkest shadow parts and the brightest light parts (the comfy middle is easy), we begin to find the serenity and joy of being.

I've found the fullness of life by courageously going where I was most afraid to go, by going into the discomfort I was trained to fear. There is vitality in all of my experiences, and being willing to be with whatever arises in my experience — even and especially the difficult emotions — is the gift of my life and my soul. And there, THERE, is where I found my wholeness and, in fact, my fullest joy.

> We don't need more connection to Spirit. Our connection to Spirit is already whole and infinite! What we really need is a deeper connection to, and compassionate understanding of, ourselves.

The most spiritual thing I can be is fully human. When I do the work . . . when you do the work, we are able to meet and know ourselves. Living this life while running a small business provides fertile soil for this epic growth adventure.

This leads me back to first grade Allison. So often when life, relationships, or business, are upsetting or frustrating me, Little Allison has been triggered and is anxious and scared. Any time our little ones show up in our life, relationships, or work, there is an opportunity for compassion, connection, and caring that leads to a deeper knowing of ourselves.

Are you doing the deep inner work of this thing called life?

# The Thief In the Night

I was terrified, completely terrified. I can see that now, but I didn't realize it then. No wonder I was depressed for most of my life. I was repressed most of my life.

Next to me at my desk sits a folder of papers from the mid-1990s. It is a collection of a few things I didn't throw out when my mom gave me an old file cabinet from the bedroom of my youth. Some of my art is in there, a university invoice from the final semester of my second senior year: $1,800 for a twelve-hour load of courses. I just noticed that the manila folder is, in my own handwriting, labeled "Song of Solomon Notes."

My stomach turns as I flip through the pages and pages of the young me trying so hard in that folder. Trying to mold myself into the perfect "Godly woman" so that the "model man" would choose me. My handwriting is pristine, tight, organized, and beautiful, actually. I am confronted with page after page of words from a book I was told was *the* one and only truth. As I read what I'd written so long ago, I can feel the tears rise up.

This folder of notes, full pages from various personal studies, brings me to my gut with grief and nausea. These were not class notes. These were personal pages from private study time. I was about twenty years old.

A contract — a full, college-ruled notebook page, I titled, My Committal:

> "I now present myself . . . Everything I am and have —
> body, mind and soul: my gifts and abilities, my time, my
> future, my home, my goods, my money, my family and

loved ones, my position and ambitions, other things that I by nature have counted as my own. I lay this on thine altar and reckon it all, from this moment, to be thine alone, and from this moment on, I believe that . . . thou dost take me, and that thou wilt continually cleanse me . . ."

What the actual brainwashed fuck?

I've never been one prone to regret the past. There is a part of me that knows: everything that happens is a part of my journey and it unfolds perfectly so that I can be here now, knowing, and loving myself. Earlier this year, when I received an official ADHD diagnosis, there was a moment of grief, but mostly, I felt absolute clarity and liberation. Many people told me there might be a period of grieving over what I'd missed because I didn't know about my neurodivergent brain. Instead, the shame lifted and there has mostly been mental freedom since. Today though, seeing these notes from a time when I was striving so hard to be some made-up woman my religion taught me I *should* be, there is deep grief and a part of me wonders, "what if?" I feel the sensation of loss and a gaping hole. I sense the forty-two years lost to a belief seared into my sweet, eight-year-old, still-forming brain as she sat criss-cross-apple-sauce on the blue, Berber carpet, near the door, watching a movie about the apocalypse called *The Thief In the Night*[17] on a TV atop a rolling cart, presented to me by a beloved teacher. I know now who the real thief is, and what was stolen.

I've been a writer for as long as I can remember. Writing in my journals, making notes upon notes of things that interested me. Even today I have nine journals stacked beside me, and a Google drive dedicated to my writing. What I see in that young twenty-year-old woman's writing tucked neatly into that manila folder broke me open.

Today I write to create, to free myself, to express. And every last page in this folder next to me, the art, the notes, the journal pages, are all an expression of trying to condition myself to be good enough, a godly woman, worthy of a godly man . . . because at eight years old, at a school my parents trusted, my third-grade teacher, and fourth, and fifth, and so on . . . showed me a movie, presented as truth, about the day Christ would return and take the good enough to heaven. A movie about a young girl who was left behind. This "Christian" horror film weaponized violent abandonment and the innocent good-enough-ness of children in service of supposed salvation.

Of course, what's funny is when I remember my "Evangelical days," I don't remember things like these study pages, and the tightness I held within myself, from the tip of my blue Bic pen up my arm, over my shoulder, creeping permanently into every cell in my body, and the wiring in my brain because of the toxic indoctrination of a socially acceptable religion. I'll tell you what I do remember, though, the day and place I renounced that religion — still afraid I'd be evaporated by a lightning bolt from the sky — at thirty-six years old.

The vague sense of being sold a load of fearful religious bullshit is gone, I now precisely see, remember, feel, and know the moment I began contorting, bending, pretending . . . and trying with every-thing I had, to be good enough. A little one's most innocent and basic fear was manipulated, and it stuck. I now know every thread of insecure attachment, every people-pleasing-good-girl drive was born on that day in that third-grade classroom. I armored up to save my very existence and to escape being abandoned by the world and the family I so loved.

# The Body Always Knows

> "And I said to my body softly,
> 'I want to be your friend.'
> It took a long breath and replied,
> 'I've been waiting my whole life for this.'"
>
> — Nayyirah Waheed

Not usually prone to allergic reactions, the day I put on my wedding dress, the one I would wear to my first wedding, my chest broke out in hives. Perhaps it really was an allergic reaction, or perhaps my body knew and was trying to tell me. Either way, the body always knows. We try to lead ourselves with our heads or with our hearts when really, the *body* is the one who knows everything.

The body knows before our conscious mind does. Yet, as young ones, most of us were taught to "think," "be smart," and "use our heads." In western culture, most of us have not been taught to listen to our bodies, even though these miraculous and complex bodies hold so much wisdom for us. Our bodies are not just the containers for our Spirit and mind, they are an integral and wise component. They are miraculous scientific excellence. The health and well-being of the mind is profoundly connected to the health and well-being of our bodies.

You have probably had an instance when you made a decision that you knew was useful and the people around you thought you were nuts. I'll bet this decision didn't make any logical sense, and yet you *knew* . . . not from your brain but from your body. Sometimes we say, "I followed my heart." Or, maybe you had the opposite experience. You made a decision, it seemed logical and everything outside of you supported this decision, but your gut told you differently. Your body knew and tried to give you some signal.

In all these years of coaching, I've heard countless stories where clients, no matter their spiritual beliefs, had a body experience that went against their minds. After the story played out, looking back and connecting back, the body always knew. The body tried to give signals. Our bodies have so much information and wisdom to share with us, if only we will turn on our awareness and attention, and listen.

How connected to your body are you? Paying deep, sensory, and intuitive attention to my body has been an important part of developing Self-trust. Our bodies always know. What if you opened the line of communication? What if you started to build a bridge to your body with the seed of trust that is already there?

# Connecting and Listening to Your Body

Each of us is different and your relationship to your body and your ways of listening to your body may be different from mine. Even if you don't currently know the language of your body, you can begin listening and learning now. My hunch is that even if you don't feel like you are actively listening right now, you have been passively listening and possibly trying to ignore it.

Taking time to slow down, breathe deeply and consciously, and scan your body in your mind's eye, will help you connect and "hear" your body's wisdom. I am obviously not a medical doctor and this is not meant to be a substitution for medical advice. I am recommending a meditative listening exercise so that you bring your mind, body, and spirit into relationship and connection with one another.

You can do this brief practice whenever you have a pause in your day, or you can set aside some time to really slow down and tune in. Here is a "slow down and really tap in" process I share with my clients. In this exercise, I will use the name Body, as if it is a specific person and part of you that can speak in words or pictures. Personifying our Body (and our emotions or thoughts) can be a useful tool in self-awareness and healing.

- Since this is an intuition exercise, remove all distractions and perhaps find a spot outside, near nature, or in your home that is clean and clutter-free. Keep all technology — computers, mobile phones, even music, out of this exercise.

- Next, sit down with a clean, large-enough pad of paper and a writing tool that feels good in your hand. Take a few deep, clearing breaths, in and out through your nose, and then set the intention to tap into and hear your Body.
- Now, draw a simple stick figure, representing Body. Head. Torso. Arms. Legs. Hands. Feet. There is no right or wrong way to draw—just trust what comes to mind.
- Next, be sure your body is positioned comfortably and your feet are flat on the ground. Bring your awareness to Body and notice where you feel any tension, thickness, or other physical sensations. Where energy is blocked, our bodies often feel heavy, tight, or sometimes itchy. Trust your first reactions and avoid over-thinking. Body will tell you. Place a mark on your stick figure and write that body part on your page as if you are labeling it.
- Scan your whole body and trust what comes up. You may have many areas where you feel discomfort; you may just have a few. Trust what comes up and note it on your page. Once you have your paper Body labeled, take a few more deep breaths. Maybe even send a thought of appreciation to Body for sharing this awareness with you.
- Now, go through each area, breathe into your heart, bringing your attention to that part of your physical body, and ask Body:

  ♡ Is there anything you want me to know or notice?

  ♡ What wisdom or information do you have for me?

  ♡ Is there a message you want me to hear?

As you attune to each of the parts that are in need of your attention, write the very first thing that comes to your mind, and trust the message you receive. Make notes on your diagram.

- Finally, take in the information you received. Breathe in the wisdom and awareness Body has for you. Take a deep breath, in through your nose, as deep as you are able, and then with a deep verbal sigh, exhale through your mouth. Your exercise is complete.

# The Chaos Is Real

The world is chaotic, isn't it? Even as I practice calm, the chaos seems inescapable at times. You know the weeks I'm talking about — the ones that come with an unusually long list of tasks to take care of. Fires to put out with down websites, and broken air conditioning in hundred degree heat. I'm an empty nester now, and yet, I'm keenly aware that some of you gorgeous people have kids, and pets, and parents you are caring for — the lists and schedules are packed.

The chaos is real. Add current events, if you pay attention to those, and I do, and it can all be tremendously overstimulating. A call for calm or peace can often feel like another "to-do" on the list. It can all be so much, and as author Matt Kahn, in his book *Whatever Arises, Love That*[18] says, our nervous systems are inflamed. I remember the first time I heard him describe that in one of his audio books I listened to while walking my dogs a few years ago. As I listened, I saw a visual when he gently spoke those words in my ears. Like the tenderness of an inflamed wound — red, swollen, not gaping or bloody, but so fucking tender due to overstimulation and inflammation.

That moment was a clear call for care and calm for my insides, no matter what was going on in my life. Calm can surprise us at times, and it must also be intentionally cultivated. Avoiding calm and presence are a sneaky way to armor up. It's easier to go fast and be frazzled, because if we internally slow down we might . . . FEEL. And to feel on top of an already inflamed nervous system could mean eruption. My body, my being, could strive and drive and outsource and avoid for only so long.

It's itchy on the way to calm — easier to stay busy. It's uncomfortable and oh so tempting to avoid.

# Crappy Creative Days

Some days are crappy creative days.

And what matters is that you sat in your practice.

You did the thing.

Maybe flow never showed up.

Perhaps the outcome is shit.


But YOU showed up

and that is what matters.

# Escape

I'm finding myself wanting to work. But My Work . . . doesn't want me today. She knows I only want to work to avoid BEING wherever and whatever I AM in this moment. She knows the subtle things I do to escape.

I remember the exact moment I crawled out of my body to avoid the pain, and yet it still hurt. Before then I was hopeful, idealistic, and I believed. After that day I was realistic. Optimistic in my head, but now I see, not in my body.

In truth, I've been a mostly-floating head.

I don't feel alone or strange though. I know so many other floating heads. We all have a storehouse of our most favorite means to disconnection, some obvious and some subtle. We whine, we wine, we eat, we go non-stop, we scroll, we binge, we "BUY NOW," we perform and excel, we care excessively for others, we froth, and fight, and flee, and fawn, we freeze.

Now I see clearly we all have been trying to escape what we can't escape. What if there is nothing to avoid? And everything to gain as we BE with whatever arises? One of my feet is firmly on the bed . . . grounded . . . and the other resting on my knee . . . there in the air. That's me lately. One foot grounded and still the other in the open air.

What's a person to do?

Eat BBQ.

# Ebb and Flow

We all have emotionally and energetically low weeks. You know what I'm talking about . . . weeks — maybe not back to back — with no motivation and frankly, shades of depression. Other times I feel aligned, peaceful, and move with joy and hope. These are cycles I have felt most of my life. I have a family history of depression and yet, at heart I am a joyful and optimistic woman. For years, I fought against these cycles when they hit. I shamed and suffered myself in my mind and that never helped the circumstance.

Growing up, I don't recall anyone in authority or leadership mindfully sharing about their ups and downs. As I stepped into more and more independence and autonomy as a young professional, I also felt my own emotional and energetic waves. Despite those waves, I held myself to the common and harsh expectations that we all hear throughout our lives:

> Keep your shit together.
> Don't cry at work.
> You are too emotional . . . suck it up.

These expectations echoed my father's demand from childhood, "Stop that crying bullshit." Emotional care and regulation was not a priority in our house growing up. While some homes are emotionally stifled, ours was often vacillating between loving, and then, suddenly volatile. What was modeled to me was free and extreme projectile emoting of strong feelings without regard to impact, but what was taught to me was, "You have to stop your feelings in my presence."

I am not a machine, Are you? Do we have on and off buttons? I am a living, breathing organism and like everything else in nature, I have cycles. I was well into adulthood when I began to learn to nurture and care for my mental and emotional cycles.

As a young professional, the book, *The Power of Full Engagement*[19] by James E. Loehr and Tony Schwartz introduced me to the concept and science of managing energy instead of time. Studies show that to be powerfully engaged and truly productive, deliberate disengagement and rest were required. This, not relentless pushing forward, was the key to high performance and personal renewal. I let this sink in. The relief that came over me was so intense, I can still remember where I was standing when I read this concept in their book. Loehr and Schwartz were studying performance in professional athletes and then translated it to the managerial and corporate world with the concepts of ninety-minute work cycles and fifteen-minute breaks.

This idea of "managing energy" made so much sense to me. I began to cultivate my own concepts of managing energy, not time, in my life. Thinking in energy rather than time felt so much more real than anything I could put on a list or on a calendar. What contributed to my energy? What depleted it? And most of all, the days when I seemed to be in ebb were a part of the process — not a problem!

I began to pay attention to my own cycles of renewal and high performance. I was hungry for the ease and success of the flow states, and I began to practice supporting myself in the times I was not in flow — times when I was tired, overwhelmed, unmotivated, and depressed. I called these ebb and flow states, and what I began to see was that, because I was a human and not a machine, like all living things, I had ebbs and flows.

I adopted a mantra for flat days as a compassionate reminder of these natural cycles. There is ebb and flow and the flow always comes back.

the FLOW always comes back ♥ Allison

This mantra isn't an excuse for slobbing around all day on the couch and tossing all responsibility (well, some days it can be). It is a call to go within, even deeper, to listen to my body, my intuition, to care for the parts that are asking for ebby-attention, and to make mindful and supportive choices based on my energy and knowing, and the needs of my parts.

# Dry Seasons

Sometimes I think the heat and humidity actually affect my energy and thinking. Thick, hot, hazy, and slow. I start to judge it. I start to judge myself and my business. And then I remember that, slow time is grow time.

My little red oak tree experienced heat stress and lost half her leaves last week. But she's not dead. It's just a hot summer season. With tender care she will revive. And so will I. Wanting it to be cool and crisp when it is hot and slow causes needless suffering.

We are not machines. Your business is not a machine. We are gardeners. We are more like nature and less like a production line.

Near my neighborhood the hay has been harvested. I know little about the actual harvesting of hay, but I make up in my mind that without the heat to dry out the grass, there would be no hay. And that dead dry grass gives sustenance to livestock. It serves a life giving purpose.

Let the season be what it is. The cool and crisp will be back soon enough.

# I'm Not Leaving You

Once upon a time, I met and married a man who was not a risk-taker. That is actually part of what I loved about him. He had the certainty and stability that I didn't have growing up. Bill was a school teacher — and one who grew up in a military family where a paycheck of a known quantity arrived every month on the same day. As a teacher, my husband had the same security of a paycheck every single month on the same day that he had in his family growing up. In my new love's world, this is how money *should* work. When we married, I moved him and his children into a home that was afforded by the money I made working for a company, and then I did something that brought uncertainty — I quit that position abruptly and jumped into the risk of starting my own small business with no guaranteed income.

Living single, my risks affected no one. Living with my husband and bonus children, my risks trembled through our home and our relatively new marriage. While stressed and overwhelmed, I was never unsure about making it work. I came from risk-takers and self-employed people, and we always made it work.

My husband was not sure at all. My choices affected his deepest needs for security and stability. His reactions to my choices affected my deepest fears of being displeasing to those I love and also my fears of being left. I really wanted to focus on building my new coaching practice, and he really wanted me to focus on finding a job that had benefits because, in his mind, it meant safety and stability, even if it wasn't as much money as I'd made before.

He was deeply frightened. I was deeply frightened. His core wounds were painfully tender. My core wounds were painfully tender.

And guess what two frightened, wounded people in a marriage do? They fight.

For a few months, I made a series of decisions from fear. I didn't want to be left again, but I wanted to make both my marriage and my baby business work. I sold a property under market value that Bill and I both loved, during the depths of the down market, just to create cash and pay down debt. I reluctantly applied for part-time jobs at Target, Starbucks, and Ikea, praying I wouldn't get them but also knowing it was what I thought Bill needed from me. For months in my head, I told myself over and over, "I just wish Bill would trust me, I just wish Bill would trust me."

A friend at the time suggested, "What about you trusting you?"

BAM! I saw it. "I just wish Bill would trust me," became "What about ME trusting me?"

A calm came over me. I knew deep in my soul that this business thing was something I had to do — it wasn't a flaky wish or a pipe dream — it was a calling and I would figure it out. All the strange turns my life had taken had led me toward a life of soul work I never even knew I wanted.

When I became still, soothed the little afraid girl within me, and then listened within to the wise woman wanting to grow and lead, I KNEW everything would be fine. I knew this was the work I came to do, even if at that moment I had no idea how exactly to make it work. I knew that if I kept moving forward, I would find a way.

I remember Bill following me up the stairs of our house. We were starting to argue again about my self-employed endeavor. I turned mid-step and was eye to eye with him (since he was on the step below me). I lifted my hand to his cheek and told him from the soundest, most grounded place of being, "I love you, and I want our marriage to work. I also know that if you are married to me NOT being me, then it will never work. I was born to do this work, to be a risk-taker and to be self-employed, and I trust myself to do it. I know it is not comfortable for you, and if it is too uncomfortable for you to be married to someone who *has* to be self-employed, we can go our separate ways. I will never say a bad thing about you. We can peacefully realize that we have different needs and divorce. It isn't what I want, and I will understand and let you go. But I have to be me. I trust me."

His shoulders relaxed and he grabbed my hand. "We'll make it work." He said.

Not long after that conversation, I got my first client. Then my second. And we never looked back. Things weren't instantly healed — we each had miles to go to soothe and resolve our own deep wounds around security and abandonment, but it really has never distressed our marriage the way it did in that season.

It isn't my place to talk about what happened in Bill's heart, and honestly, he doesn't remember this happening. I do. It was monumental for me. I know that at that moment, in my heart and life, I had to choose me. Not from a selfish place, but from a centered-in-SELF place. If I really wanted to be loved completely and deeply for being me, then I had to trust myself to actually BE me instead of contorting and bending myself to some likable version of who I thought I should be.

At that moment, I trusted myself enough to lose my marriage, and I ended up taking a step toward healing my marriage. My trust in myself seemed to rub off on Bill. The more I stood in my own center, the more relaxed he became. As I trusted myself more and confidently moved forward, Bill also became more trusting and encouraging.

I began to really get what ownership meant in my life. Owning my power, my desire, and especially my own needs. I couldn't ever get from others what I wasn't willing to give and grow in myself.

# A Renewed Commitment to UN-

Unconventional

Unfiltered

Uncertified

Untamed

Untraditional

Unsaved

Unruly

Unexpected

Unauthorized

Unnerving

Unorthodox

Unburdened

Unarmored

Deconstructed

De-systematized

Done with the bending for your comfort and pleasure

Your unconscious bias assumes that in all this

there is mal-intent,

or evil sin

because someone,

somewhere,

said:

follow the rules

don't disrupt the status quo

be afraid

be controlled
hell and separation awaits
be anything but your unique and holy self (because I am afraid and
it is easier to control you than to meet my own consuming fear)

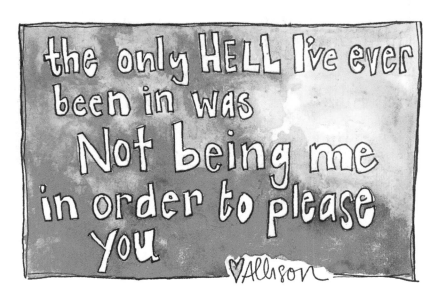

I may be too much for you
and my too-muchness
is just right for me.

I AM Sovereign
I AM Wild & Holy

I AM Free
simply because I am — completely to the edges, ALL of me.

PART 4

# Compassion

# Self-Compassion

True vulnerability and authenticity require extreme self-compassion. I know. You hear self-compassion blah blah blah all the time. When was the last time you had to practice it, though?

Recently, a podcast episode on which I was a guest came out. I listened, and part of me loved it. But a louder part of me was mortified and ashamed that I rambled and meandered and babbled — I just kept talking — on someone else's platform. The host was so gracious. And she acknowledged it was longer than most of her guest podcasts, but in the end, she didn't filter me at all. I felt honored. I was also both ashamed and embarrassed.

As I unpack that a little, I also realize that I was feeling the vulnerability hangover of exposure, and a little lost as intense self-criticism comes up. I'm meeting all of these with self-compassion. So much self-compassion.

I see you Fears and Insecurities. I see you wanting to do a good job while also spilling over the edges of life. I even see the deepest fears and concerns of "You are doing it wrong" and how your heart aches to be both fully free and still accepted. I see your desire to be adored. I am here for you.

What I tell these parts of me is, "I can't promise you won't be rejected by others. Dear One, I will never reject you. I'm so sorry for the times in the past that I did. I'm here for you now, and I won't leave you. I fully accept you to the edges and beyond. What else would you like to tell me? I'm listening."

The little parts of me still feel discomfort but they are beginning to experience that they are held in compassionate presence instead of rejection and criticism. A new layer of trust is built.

Where can you give yourself compassion? Where can you meet the inner critics or shamers and just connect lovingly with them — not to *fix* them but to hold them in your sacred self-compassion?

# Gentle Attention

Starting with gentle attention to some areas of tenderness seems just where I need to be today: compassionate awareness of parts of me where my drive is stronger than my physical energy; soft presence and recognition of all the parts showing up as I make my way through this morning.

Some parts are anxious, some are hopeful, some are sleepy and want to check out, and some ache with longing.

There is a world inside me and inside you. For so long I exiled so many of these parts to the dark, hidden corners, that I never really knew all of me. Until now, only certain parts were allowed space in my system. Some parts were highly esteemed for their functions and abilities, and others were pressed down because of their fears and tears.

Now, I'm in a new relationship with ALL parts of me. All of me is welcome. Building trust and connection with all of me is creating a deep and grounded shift.

> Calm.
> Compassionate.
> Connected.
> Curious.
> Creative.
> Confident.
> Clear.
> Courageous.

It feels good to be able to hold it all . . . even when it all feels like too much. I'm sending you some of these energies.

# Frothing

Frothing is a term I made up during an experience with a friend who was grieving the loss of her dad. Listening to her, I knew that she was standing in the shitty pain of grief and loss. And my experience of her was that instead of feeling that empty pain and loss, she was scooping up the shit she was standing in and dramatically frothing it all over herself. The froth and drama, even though miserable, wasn't as unbearable as grief.

Growing up in chaos, drama was the baseline for me. For many years, the drama was the tempo I returned to. Just when I thought I had found true calmness and ease, I would step into avoidance of the deep pain within me, and then, you know where that took me — froth. Let's stir up some shit as a distraction! When I was little, I did it by picking fights with my little sister, because it was easier to argue with her than to feel my deep desire for connection and friendship with her. For years I did this with money, earning, and spending. I did it by not saving for taxes and then needing to make the cash for the tax bill in a short amount of time.

While not technically defined as one of the nervous systems responses by the clinicians and psychologists (fight, flight, freeze, and fawn), frothing, for me, is totally a sign of my dysregulated nervous system and one of my ineffective coping mechanisms and protector parts.

I am learning to release drama about things that just aren't that important. Seeing my friend that day a few years ago was a potent mirror. Admittedly, I thought I *really* had released my frothing and drama. Of course, because I'm human, in real time, I haven't fully released my hold on the froth and the drama. I still fall into its trap.

I literally volunteered for drama recently. Facepalm is real, y'all. (This book won't dare let me write without a lived experience.) What was my trap? I have been grieving. So what did I do rather than meet my grief? I freaked the EFF out and agreed to foster a traumatized dog, of course.

Grief is a mystery to me — my whole being avoids it. Anticipatory grief is thick, too. The first time I ever saw a therapist, in my twenties, was the time I moved away from my parents to Colorado. I was overwhelmed with fear of them dying some day.

Grief touches everyone. It comes to some in natural order, and to others in what seems the most unfair ways. Lately, as I do this deep work of meeting all my parts, I've felt thick with sadness, loss, confusion, heartbreak, and grief. So many grief parts are showing up from so many ages and stages of my life, including the present moment.

♡ Parents aging, declining, a stroke, a hospital stay . . . grief.

♡ Helping parents decide to sell their home of fifty-two years, my childhood home, full of lives lived and memories, and stuff. The great downsize. Dad's falls, Mom's falls. Watching as fifty-two years of things get packed up or tossed out. Being in this stage of life, in the end-season of my parents' lives . . . grief.

♡ Five kids working to help parents downsize, with all the old family patterns and wounds. Grief.

♡ My own two beloved dogs were diagnosed with fatal conditions and the stress of managing their palliative care . . . grief.

♡ The releasing and loss of cherished relationships, some fading away, and others abruptly ending. Owie. Grief.

♡ My experience of our country, the extreme divided politics, an insurrection mostly ignored, overturning of Roe v. Wade, the demise of voting rights, elementary children massacred while in school in my home state, inflation driven by war, greed, and toxic capitalism, a disintegrating healthcare system, the threat of our nation becoming an authoritarian Christian theocracy where women and anyone other than alt-right-and-white don't have rights, mother earth scorched by climate change, and being called a fearmonger for being concerned. HOLY fucking grief.

My whole body is tight with the pain and pressure. My usual remedies are weak with the extent of my dread. I had a high blood pressure reading last weekend for the first time ever. And so what do I do? I raise my hand when the rescue group I work with sends me a photo of a little dog with an injured eyeball, "Can you foster this little dude?"

"Yes, *clearly* yes, because I *obviously* have time and space and a well regulated nervous system to take on a traumatized dog I know very little about, and *especially* yes, because it will disrupt the peace I currently have at home with my own crew. Bring it on."

Froth away.

Froth to try to control something because there is so much I can't control.

Froth because I crave calm, love, and reciprocation after rejection.

Froth to take on work that will dissociate you from the intense sorrow you feel.

Anything to move away from the pain, instead of compassion-ately toward it.

Hello Frothing, I see you.
I won't leave you.
I am here for you.

This is what we do. It's what I do. It's what we've been trained to do. Western society does not do discomfort, and we certainly don't do grief. I made a choice, from my frothing place, I brought the foster home and named him Harry B. Styles. My choice blew through my peaceful home like a west Texas tornado, causing damage for my dogs, for my husband, our relationships, for me, and for Harry.

This choice, and a few others in the last season, were made from a completely hijacked nervous system grasping for control. This isn't mindset. This isn't cognitive. It's old conditioning, and I wobble intensely even though I'm slowly moving through this journey of feeling it all. Sometimes it is glorious, and sometimes it is miserable.

I can say I screwed up, which doesn't matter after the choice has been made, or I can surrender to the awareness of what is. Now I can SEE. The awareness didn't come until after the fights and tears, sleepless nights, and full-on TILT, and meltdown. I said yes to a dog who is all up in his nervous system, just like I am. He needs way more space and decompression than all of my previous fosters (so grateful for the gentle, compassionate, and skilled behaviorist that helped me see this).

I am starting to really get that the state of my nervous system needs to come first. After thirty years of personal growth and fifty years of living, I finally get that it isn't my being or my mindset that is primary. It is only ever my nervous system that must be compassionately regulated in order to begin anything.

Today, here and now, the practice I desire to metabolize — to embody — with every cell in my being, is to just be with my body and breath, moment by moment. Nothing cognitive can happen when we aren't regulated, when we are frothing, or freezing, or fighting, or fawning, or fleeing. *This* is the work of "respond versus react." It's in the body, not the brain.

Practice. Practice. Practice.

Compassion. Compassion. Compassion.

Harry B. Styles, you little one eyed, black Boston terrier baby, once again, a dog has come to help me learn to be a better and whole human. I see you. I won't use you to bypass grief. Instead, together we will learn how to get back to our bodies so that we can thrive again. Thank you for showing me the way.

# Let All Your Edges
# Be Frayed

I see you trying to clean up the edges,
shifting, and adjusting, trying to make everything just so.
Fidgeting and squirming in your body and in your thinking.
Reaching for some perfection that doesn't exist.

Come, let all your edges be frayed.
Let all your edges be frayed.

Let's just be here.
HERE.

# Be Soft With the Hard

I spent most of my life as a professional bypasser. I bypassed so well that I had no idea I was doing it, and I wondered why I struggled with chronic and clinical depression. Pressing hard emotions down and away will do that. When I sense into those depressive episodes from the past, I can also feel how my head tried to disconnect from my body, inching above me into the spiritual, ethereal, transcendent realms, while my feet were still stuck on the ground. Can you see the visual in your mind? This unconscious disassociation left a gaping hole in the middle where the core of my body should be. And it felt exactly like that.

Through an IFS lens, I now see how I was living a version of the *Princess and the Pea*, by Hans Christian Andersen, with her stack of mattresses. You see, I have a handful of tiny, tender, green sweet peas — these old original hurting inner child parts that are hidden away — Exiles are what we call them in IFS. My exiled, "sweet peas" are the parts of me that hold pain and trauma, rejection, deep wounds, and shame. They are innocent, and at one time, had a vitality and eagerness. After woundings, however, they've been isolated and pressed down, yet they are still tender and vulnerable and full of painful emotions and beliefs.

Other parts of me, my protectors, are like the mattresses, piled up and covering the tender little peas, hoping that the mattresses will offer protection from feeling the pain in life. The mattresses are either: Manager Parts (responsive and proactive parts that try to run daily life and give the illusion of control and safety); or, Firefighter Parts (reactive parts that strive to prevent pain by numbing, bypassing, outsourcing, and distancing from difficult feelings).

need for approval
Rage & throwing shit
Making $$$$$ Money
Solving problems
co-dependence
being "POSITIVE"
anxiety
over·thinking
DEPRESSION
Lovers · Sex · boys
intellectual Smarts
drinking · food
Religion · Spirituality
achievement at
Being a GOOD GIRL

♡AllisonCrow

What I have come to realize is that each protective mattress, each coping behavior, had benevolent intent to *protect* me, so that I would never feel so hurt again. But, with each layer of hiding and protecting my sweet inner peas, I got further away from all of me. The discomfort became unbearable, until meeting these parts of me became the only thing I hadn't tried in my quest to feel "good."

No one really teaches us how to feel and be with difficult emotions. We are so rough with them. We are so critical and judging and shaming, that it makes life so much harder than it needs to be. To feel good, we have to learn to be soft with what is hard.

UNARMORED

Be SOfT with the Hard ♡Allison

"What is one thing that was not tolerated in your family growing up?" was a question I heard recently. The first thing that rose up in my memories was emotions. Any and all emotions were both suppressed and stuffed, and then — after a period of time — they exploded like a jack-in-the-box. Without realizing it, I pushed everything to the frayed edges and pulled all the energy into my head and ideas, leaving a pile of protective mattresses covering my peas.

I now know that my body is wise, and that my emotions, all the mattresses, and my tender peas, all have information for me. They are all worthy and waiting for my presence and connection. All they needed from the beginning was my compassionate care and validation. Feeling is an actual skill that can be learned. Time on task builds self trust and emotional capacity.

There is both a language and somatic sensation of all these emotions:

- ♥ Doubt/Fear
- ♥ Over-functioning
- ♥ Procrastination
- ♥ Comparison
- ♥ Overthinking
- ♥ Grief/Loss/Disappointment

I think SO much. I have so many thinking and problem-solving parts. This has helped me be very accomplished and successful in work. Yet these parts torment me at times. They can be helpful. They also can loop in what feels like an infinite way. Oh, the ways we find to squirm out of feeling the sensations of these difficult emotions.

Being hard, I view these emotions and coping skills as a problem to solve. "Just move the mattresses!" Being soft with the hard, I remember that none of these thinking parts can be cared for in my head, but only in the space and physicality of my body and breath. Only through reestablishing self-connection, presence, and calm, will these protectors begin to relax. Only through compassion and an actual relationship will our inner system become safe enough to transform these old ways.

Judgment, self-criticism, shame, blame, guilt, never softened these pains. Only soft has, only soft can. Be soft with the hard.

# Smart Parts and Other Exhausted Delusions of Certainty

For so many years I've been too smart for my own good. I'm a life-long student and always will be. My intellectual prowess has always given me a sense of safety and security. For most of my life, this was an unconscious characteristic, and now I see that this was the anchor I hitched my being to so that I would feel safe in a chaotic life. I see how my intellect helped me solve problems, thrive after divorce, and create a successful coaching practice. It served me until there were glitches that my intelligence couldn't solve. I now see places where my nervous and psychological systems still wig-out, because they don't feel safe or certain.

In 2015, a friend and meditation mentor, Dr. Jeffrey Rutstein, asked me if I had experienced childhood trauma.[20] My first response was, "No." In so many ways, I had a really good childhood. I had very loving and involved parents. I went to private school and we had a boat and a pool. My parents attended every basketball game I played in. I grew up with a community of neighborhood kids, I was on the softball and swim teams. We took hill country family trips, and it seemed we were always together. Because my life wasn't the kind of violent life that was depicted on after school TV specials, my brain made up that there was no trauma.

Um, YES . . . There was trauma at home and at school and at church. I had a physically traumatic bike injury in fourth grade. There was alcoholism, verbal abuse, emotional uncertainty, neglect, financial chaos, food insecurity, emotional manipulation, and religious trauma. My sweet mom had a debilitating disability, and gave birth to four kids in five years, and I had a lot of adult responsibilities way too soon. I'm Gen X! Of course there was trauma. I also had traumatic experiences with each set of grandparents, one wealthy and one poor. I was traumatized and threatened with damnation and abandonment at my religious school.

Obviously, my parents were doing the best they could with the tools they had — they both had traumatic childhoods, and frankly, ALL of us have had trauma in our lives.

Some of my obvious beneficial expressions of this chaos have been:

- Extremely creative, imaginative, and artistic
- Valuing people and relationships
- Highly developed sensory and intuitive skills
- Attuned to the emotional needs of others
- Kick-ass strategic thinking and problem-solving skills
- Independence and leadership initiative
- Entrepreneurial spirit, driven
- Originality and willingness to be a maverick and take risks

Some of my obvious difficult expressions of this chaos have been:

- Perpetual hyper-vigilance
- People-pleasing
- Vague boundaries
- Verbal abuse
- Emotional eruption and rage
- Over-functioning
- Over-debting
- Codependency
- Conflict avoidance

- Cutting people out of my life completely and quickly when it hurts
- Clinical depression and anxiety
- Excruciating fear of rejection and excessive need for validation
- ADHD and masking behaviors
- Hyper-independence

Slowly and gently, I began to see the places where unhealed trauma still lived in my cells, my bones, and my psychology. I began to notice and recollect stories, not as a victim, but as an aware being. Oh . . . of course, that had an impact on you, and here's where and how it shows up as an adult.

I'm so grateful for gentle teachers, like Jeffrey, and Chris Zydel, my therapists, and countless authors and teachers I've never actually met in person. They have led me in a compassionate discovery and acceptance of *all* of me. I am in love. (Compassion and relationship were key here — no "ass-kicking" — that would just have been more trauma.)

These teachers taught me not to just "know thyself," but to *relate* to myself, connect, and BE with all the parts of me, with loving-kindness. They have also taught me that my nervous system and body are a major part of the process and healing. This is why, from an intellectual standpoint, these old wounds would not, and could not, be healed.

Almost everyone I know has joined me at some point in saying, "I know it in my head . . . But I just can't seem to XYZ . . ." This is why: It can't be healed with a mindset shift. I love coaching. And coaching without embodiment — nervous system knowledge, and trauma-informed care — is just a Band-Aid on a festering wound. And that's OK, until it isn't.

You'll know. You will KNOW in your being when it's time to really go full-body and deeper emotionally into your system. At age fifty, I can see it all coming together. I can connect the dots of the past so clearly. It's all so perfect. Even the trauma. It's made me this tapestry of a human that I so sweetly and tenderly love, connect to, and intellectually understand.

While I'm excited about the future, what is BEST is being in this moment, on my back porch. I am here *now*, with myself, with my story, and with this moment (and two panting boxer dogs). I am safe being me. I am safely opening my heart. I am safe here and now.

I wish this peace for anyone who desires to have it.

# Breathe Bigger
# Than Your Parts

For people who subconsciously lead with their heads and thinking parts, we need to remember that compassion is more than an attitude or set of thoughts. It is a somatic and energetic way of being with ourselves, from inside the core of our bodies. Through the entryway of conscious breathing, we can begin to "breathe bigger than our parts,"[21] as one of my IFS teachers, Kay Gardner, says. She brought so much compassion to our training — it's one of her SELF gifts. We know that sometimes little ones need softness in a hard world, but we adults need softness, too. The softness of compassion heals.

Breathing bigger than your parts works both as a recurring mindfulness practice (I call mine hand on heart, hand on belly time — somewhat like meditation and breathwork combined), and as a go-to skill for difficult times. I am creating the intentional habit and skill of doing my best to remember this when I get dysregulated. I've set up reminders and systems in my day — my family members know when to gently let me know I'm in TILT — and in my work with clients, we are creating community that is practicing nervous system awareness and regulation as a foundation.

So often my compassion gets stuck in my head, where it comes from a thinking part place instead of true loving SELF-energy and Source. Taking the time to put a hand on my heart and another hand on my belly, and focus my awareness and energy on my core, breathing bigger than all my parts, is soothing, settling, and healing. It is an energy connected through mind, body, and spirit, with a regulated nervous system. For me, it is a coming home, and makes space in what can often be a chaotic internal system.

SELF Energy, or Source Energy — the DIVINE YOU, is always present. Like the sun in the sky, it's always there, but the conditions may make it hard to sense. Mental managers run amok in control mode, or firefighters run amok in defend and distract mode, and they cut off our connection to SELF. I often mentally understand this. I can be compassionate with myself, but until I remember to go deeper inside myself (mind/body/spirit), slowly breathing bigger, and asking my problem-solving parts to step back, not much changes.

There is a saying in IFS, "Speak *for* parts, not through parts." Taking the mental and somatic space by speaking *for* parts also makes a way for SELF energy to expand.

"I am anxious," this is speaking *from* a part — it has a mental effect on my state of being, claiming it as my truth. I love I AM statements, but I never could reconcile my truth around just tossing aside my difficult experiences by shoving them into a positive I AM statement.

Claiming I AM PEACE when a part of me doesn't feel peace at the moment, frankly, feels like shit!

Compassion, and speaking *for* parts says, "A part of me is feeling anxious." In that space of both slight separation and witnessing, compassion comes forth. Here, I can remember that I am not my parts, they are a part of me, and that I am the wise loving leader they need. I can move from parts-led to SELF-led. From this space, more compassion connects with the anxious parts, and now I am the loving presence and guide for all parts of me, without having to reject any part of myself.

What follows is the space to get to know what these parts of me are deeply longing for, and what they are afraid of. So often, it is connection and compassion, instead of the harshness of "pushing through."

# Melancholy Mornings

Some mornings just feel so heavy. I wake up with a cloud of forgetting.

# You Are Doing It Wrong

Does anyone else have an old trauma-based sensitivity to this phrase? My siblings and I had enough of these moments with our parents when we were young that it became a "family saying."

I remember a time as a family, we got into the car after my brother's baseball game, and the first thing my dad mentioned was the grounder my brother missed, and how he could adjust his form when extending his glove. "You're doing it wrong" was what my brother, and all of us listening, heard. Upset and deeply hurt he replied, "Yeah, Dad, but what about the two home runs I hit?"

I have been a puppet to these strings. And I'm certain I've expressed, "You are doing it wrong" to others more times than I wish. I'm so very sorry. One of my great paradoxes is both losing who the world told me I should be (and still does tell me), and discovering my own authentic way. Unhooking from the world's expectations and grounding to my center often still seems wrong, because it is never enough.

At the micro level, I'm fucking it all up — I'm sure of that. At the macro level, though, I remember this present moment. I remember that I am a speck of fleshy dust on a rock, floating through infinite space. I am a tiny five foot nine coagulation of matter with thumbs typing on a device with a screen that allows me to see my words in front of me, rather than swirling around in my head.

Yet, none of it ever seems good enough. Inside of me or outside of me. I'll never be a good enough white, cis-gendered, colonized, un-racist, un-indoctrinated, un-Christianized, lib-t#@^, socialist-commie-woman, and you'll never be a good enough whatever you failed at in the world's eyes. Oh, and we can also add "non-vegan" to this list now after some woman decided she could help me by telling me on a social media post how much suffering I ingest when I eat the meat of animals. Thanks lady, for proving my point.

None of us are doing it right, and we are all doing it better than everyone around us (in our eyes). It's exhausting.

I see your mess, and I see your perfection. I see you doing it "wrong," and I see you doing it the best you are capable of. I see myself doing the same.

I spent most of my fifty years trying to be better. Do right and good and care in the right ways. And it has NEVER been enough. At the end of the day, here I am with ME. Just me. My right way can only ever be good enough for me. It has NEVER lived up to YOUR (whoever you are) expectation. I'm working on letting your right be good enough for you. Do our rights/our correctness EVER meet in the same place? Maybe for a moment. But after that moment, another moment happens and shows us our separateness, and wrongness.

The "shoulds" rip us in two, and we both lose. We both end up wrong. Again, It's exhausting. No matter what I preach — it is only right now and it only has to be enough for me, because it will never be enough for whoever *them* is. And it won't ever be right for you. What a complicated world we live in, with the ever present threat of un-belonging. (I've also read that this is very much a white woman thing — and could be — I am a white woman.)

Un-belonging. This is the hook that freezes us, or fights us, or fawns us due to the threat of disconnection, rejection, or, heaven forbid, left behind in the apocalypse. Other than life and death, this is the one thing we all have in common — the innate need to belong. I'm tired of trying to belong in a way that makes you happy while I lose me. I'm tired of trying to belong in a way that works for you, but not for me.

I'm allowed to center myself. You are allowed to center yourself. You are the center of your universe, and I am the center of mine.

The cycle goes on and we retreat within — each of us trying to rip another from their center for our own security. It is exhausting.

And so for today, I will just be here with my dog and my words and expression, and the air touching the bottom of my feet, and my bra feeling too tight, and my throat a bit itchy. This is just where I am. Belonging to only my own sweet soul and SELF of me, has to be enough.

> I breathe and check-in . . .
> and it is enough.

PS: I can smell that my sweet dog is dying. It's in his breath. Because that is what life is. It is living and loving, and then death.

I will be ok. I do have a lot of deep sadness. I won't pretend it isn't there. Some days it is heavy. I share to normalize this for you, and for me, and for the people who tell me my willingness to express some of this difficult and unpresentable human experience helps.

At the end of the day, expressing myself always brings me back to hope. Other systems I've been a part of — toxic religion, toxic spirituality, toxic coaching — tell me not to be a "victim." I'm not a victim. I'm a human. I'm a woman of range, here to feel it all, and I'm done denying my humanness in service of someone else's pleasure and comfort.

I'm here to live in the paradoxes of creativity and death, caring and hopelessness, effort and failure. I'm here to explore all the way to the edges of being human. I'm not here to escape the systems. I'm here to be in them and to regenerate my own system within them. Some days that is easy and glorious, and other days it is hard. I no longer need it to be easy. I just need it to be *real*.

# Reason Versus Fault

Being in the coaching industry is fabulous. Being in the coaching industry also taught me a plethora of bypass mindset tools.

A heavy and unhelpful chunk of what was unhelpful was the toxic positivity and spirituality. All these tools helped me to feel good in the moment, but they also encouraged me to shove down so much that really needed to be released. And to be released, it needed to be witnessed.

Coaching is often a "no complaints" culture, a culture of "gratitude is the answer," and you have either a "growth mindset or a fixed mindset." Because my sweet soul wanted to belong, and because those ideas helped me avoid difficult emotions, I gladly went along. And, shit gladly built up in my body until it broke down. Shit gladly built up in my emotional being, until the inner three-year-old in me flooded me and took over in the middle of adult, business, ordinary-conflict conversations that could have been mostly benign.

When I respectfully started listening to my complaints, they gave me valuable information.

Shame is heavy. I've been taught that the energy of shame vibrates near death — and perhaps I believe it. Somatically, it most certainly feels that way. In the past, any complaint I had came with a heaping side of shame. Any difficult emotion I experienced came with shame. My own neurodivergent ways of processing (before I knew I was neurodivergent) came with so much shame. Through compassionate witnessing practices of my parts via IFS, I was able to explore behavior patterns and the protective trauma responses that tripped me up as a grown woman.

One day, my sweet mom, who follows my social media faith-fully, said, "I'm so sorry for all the trauma we caused when you were a child."

My immediate and sincere response was this: "Mom, I don't find any fault, only reason."

This distinction settled into my being and body — not an ounce of blame or shame. When I finally began to witness parts of me that had complaints, parts of me that were begging for my attention instead of being meditated away — and even shame — these parts began to share stories, and show me exact points in time when certain behavioral and coping mechanisms were set-off in my system.

When I listened with care to my complaints, shame softened. Only the world told me that complaining was bad. Only believing what the world told me about being either a victim or a growth-minded human caused me to suffer.

Reason helped me see the puzzle pieces and track back to the most natural and biological equations that launched a thousand unconscious and protective behaviors, in me, and in others. Instead of finding fault with myself and others, I was able to see the reason. With reason, compassion flooded in.

Thus, the more I meet myself, the less I want to punch other people in the face.

Behavioral science is so cool.

# Punching People
# In the Face

Here is one of my personal mantras . . .

What sets you off? What triggers you? Doesn't it always seem to happen at the worst times?

In much of the coaching and personal development world, we've been chronically taught to "change our thinking" or some other form of positivity bypass. How does that work for you in the heat of a tussle with your spouse, or an upset client?

Leading ourselves in moments where we are triggered can be tough . . . and there are skills to develop this SELF-leadership. These are the skills of unblending, welcoming and moving toward, instead of away from, our troubling and intense parts. Intentionally spending time with these parts BEFORE they get triggered is a practice that can help.

"The way we relate to our parts translates directly to how we relate to people when they resemble our parts."

— Richard C. Schwartz, PhD.[22]

# No More

I was once told by a colleague that, perhaps, I was too soft and that my clients needed more shoving and pushing.

I can be clear, direct, and compassionate. I will not relent with compassion. I won't bulldoze over the roots of the pains and problems for a quick and temporary symptom fix. The world uses force to contort our being — and I won't do it.

I'm here for the deep work. I am here for the work that truly creates lasting change and self-trust. I'm here for helping my clients reclaim authority, SELF-trust, and SELF-leadership. This means I have to claim my own authority, SELF-trust, and SELF-leadership.

No more leading from these parts:

> Over or under-functioning parts
> Fear of being left or rejected parts
> Avoiding grief parts
> People-pleasing parts
> Good girl parts
> Shame, blame, and guilt parts
> Need to know everything parts
> Overthinking parts
> Numbing or disassociated parts
> Fuck-you raging parts
> Doubting parts

I know the quick fixes, fast results, and big cash are alluring. My clients have gone that route and now see and feel in their bodies that they want full-body success on their own terms, by their own definition. Success is what they want, not just in the bank account or the brain, but in every cell in their bodies.

PART 5

# Curiosity

# The Pressure to Always Be Nexting

Everywhere I look there is the pressure to get to the NEXT "level." Next this, next that. No celebration, move on . . . bigger, bigger, bigger. Hustle, Hustle, HUSTLE. Scale. Accelerate.

How does that make your body feel? Seriously, check in . . . feel . . . sense. Is there lightness and excitement, or is there constriction and a pit of nausea in your tummy? Either one is OK, and if you sense a constriction, keep reading. Or, keep reading if you just want to hear a funny story. I'm here to tell you there is another way.

When I was a school teacher (yes, for five years in a small Catholic school in Austin, Texas), I was asked to be the coach of the seventh/ eighth-grade boy's basketball team. There was an A-Team that was all about results and achievement. And the B-Team — well, we were out to have fun and just do a good job. I practiced with my B-Team, and I coached more than basketball to these young men. I coached life and heart and soul.

My guys LOVED being on my team. We won. We had fun. The A-Team guys were drawn to us. They would come and tell me, "Coach Crow, I wanna be on your team." I asked why and was met with answers about the energy and fun we were having and how there just wasn't that crushing pressure to perform. Also, we were winning. I wasn't an asshole coach, I was firm and boundaried, but willing to smile and enjoy our experience that season.

When I think about what I want for my work — for my life — what comes up first is a clear knowledge of what I don't want: striving, hustle, constriction, comparisonitis, overachieving, exhaustion, and panic attacks at 1:00 a.m. or 4:00 a.m. What is it about this life that we are conditioned to NEXT ourselves? Next, Next, Next. Like there is some station to get to on this journey of life. And if we happen to get somewhere, we must get to the NEXT level or the NEXT phase.

Being a professional life and business coach, as well as into personal growth, these fields are wrought with Nexting, expansion, the push for growth, and getting to the next level. It's the paradox I live and work in. Nexting makes me feel constricted. Unfolding feels yummy.

In my early years of coaching, and then going out on my own, I efforted and strove, and created, and served, and strategized, and coached, and planned and implemented and hustled — until my soul was dreary and parched.

And then, I started painting. Playing. It was like the B-Team all over again. Let's do a good job, have fun, be playful, and create. More is not better, better is better. And, I'm not gonna lie, the last five years of my work have been the MOST fun, profitable, and easy.

Even with that acknowledgement and that wisdom, I'm still tempted. Every day I'm tempted to MORE, to NEXT. Parts of me are hooked into and allured by the invisible messaging from outside that tempts me . . . parts of me are poking from within . . . their knowledge and skill and thirst for more are insatiable.

One day, my husband told me:

> "Allison, you know I chose you and love you because you
> are into personal and spiritual growth. And, you work
> soooo hard at it. I don't work at it at all, and I still grow."

Dang, he is right. I married a man who doesn't do any "self-help." I married fucking YODA™. Just like nature — the trees don't hustle yet they still grow. The flowers don't NEXT, and they still bloom. I want to be like nature and flow, and not like the machine I was or am tempted to be. I don't mind inspired work and action, and I must choose unfolding instead of NEXTING every single day. For me, there is a fine line. I'm not talking about sitting on the couch eating bonbons and waiting for life to show up in some magical, fantasy manifestation. I am talking about dreaming, playing, and following the feel-good of inspired action, the support of nourishing practices, and SELF-generated creativity and clarity.

the flowers do not "NEXT" they still BLOOM

♥Allison

Being prosperous is important to me; financially and emotionally. Being well and happy is important to me. And I'm determined to listen within instead of to mass media and the majority of my coachy biz social media feeds. I'm figuring out how to do that one day at a time.

There is NOTHING wrong with the A-Team — I'm just not that hungry. It is breaking my body, my spirit, to even try to be on the A-team anymore. I am enough. BE Team . . . I'm in. All In. To each their own.

We need more BE Team people. We will use creativity, fun, and love to meet our challenges. We will help one another remember that we don't have to be striving, hustling overachievers. Together, we will create a new definition of success.

# Faith Versus Trust

Have faith.
Believe.
Just trust.

Those words in my compliant, naive ears lifted me higher for years. These words can soothe for a moment, but swallow those words, let them become one with your cells, and take root in the marrow of your bones, and they will steal your innate power. The exact opposite of what I was promised they would do.

faith
/fāTH/
*noun*
Complete trust or confidence in someone or something.

Eighteen years after my first husband left me, I realized I'd lost more than a marriage. My divorce lawyer once said to me, "Kids or not, divorce is splitting one life into two. It isn't easy."

But it wasn't just the divorce. When he walked out that door, all the hopes and a whole lot of fucking dreams died. Yes, my life took a hard left turn and into a direction wildly different and more delightful than even my young-girl dreams, and yes, it eventually worked out. Only recently have I seen and been able to gently pick up what the real damage of my divorce was, though.

Yes, I lost a man I thought would be the father of my children and the love of my life until death-do-us part. I lost most of my Christian friends because divorce scares the shit out of the so-called-holy, like a contagious and deadly disease. These days, divorce and being liberal seem to be the equivalent of the leprosy of biblical times.

What I really lost was my precious hope and faith. I had faith that I would be loved, that I would be held in good times and bad. I had accumulated thirty years of believing that I would be a mother of children born from the love of my husband and me. I had faith in the stories I was told and sold.

That woman — for thirty years — practiced, preached, and culti-vated faith. She believed that faith and trust were the same things. But, while faith could be instant, trust takes time. A few years after my divorce, while discussing a disappointing date with one of my friends, bewildered by my fast faith in the men I dated, he said to me, "Allison, you trust too fast. Trust takes time."

FML. He was right.

My worldview was FAITH. Faith in something other than myself to be creating and discerning. Faith that life would turn out because it was in God's hands. My faith was an idyllic fantasy sold to me by my religion, "Just have faith and trust, and you will be saved. God will take care of it all."

The faith of my youth kept me from being in my body. Faith was easier to live in than the pain of the things of a human life that fucking hurt. The delusion of faith was my escape from both reality and responsibility.

The faith of my youth kept me with my head in the clouds and swayed by the wind. The faith of my youth was the feel-good marketing of the religious systems — no more real than polar bears drinking Diet Coke and wearing cute, red scarves at Christmas time. The faith of my youth was a flat-out lie.

I don't believe there is a God who plays chess with our lives. We have more power than that. And less. More power because it wasn't a higher power's strategic chess moves that had me blindly trust the people in my life who threw a thousand red flags my way before they hurt me. Responsibility. Less power, because there are just some things we aren't able to see coming. There are some things that just happen. Reality.

You've seen the meme. You are responsible only for what you can control. As far as what is out of your control? You can only be responsible for how you respond.

I've since lived my own personal distinction between faith and trust. For me, trust is now something that is built over time through evidence. Trust requires experimentation and testing. Trust takes time.

Holy awareness within! Trust is the scientific fucking method!

Step 1: Hypothesis.

Step 2: Experimentation.

Step 3: Observe, collect, and assess data.

Step 4: Make adjustments and experiment again.

Step 5: Do enough experiments and collect enough data to either prove or disprove your hypothesis.

I'm really not as cynical as you may think I am. In fact, I believe I have more realistic hope than ever, thanks to testing and experimenting. Allowing trust to be a process of experience and embodied valuation pulls me out of made-up mental fuckery. Even when I don't have evidence that I can trust, I can see for myself the evidence that supports the clear lack of certainty.

I *mostly* haven't lost my belief in the spiritual and faith in the unseen. I just don't confuse faith and trust anymore. Part of me is grounded in the mysticism of the boundless oneness and connection of this literally-infinite universe. I am open to her magic and miracles. Another part of me is rooted firmly in the Earth and in the experimentation of life. I, an infinite soul, am here in my miraculous human body. And when my experiments fail, I am more and more willing to take those failures less personally. Once again, I find myself in the comfort of both/and.

PS: The first image from NASA's James Webb Space Telescope was released recently: Webb's First Deep Field[23] is the tiniest slice of our vast universe. It is the deepest and sharpest image of distant galaxies ever captured. Even seeing the image on my small phone screen left me sitting with holy perspective, and my sense of faith was expanded. The miracle of our existence in this vast universe full of galaxies touches my heart. Tears rise up.

# Bet On Yourself
# Over and Over

When I was about eleven, I had a funny fantasy of being discovered for being remarkably unique. One day I begged my brother to let me do his chore of mowing the yard because I was sure that a limo with a Hollywood producer would be driving down my out-of-the-way neighborhood street in Austin, Texas, and be stunned and enchanted by the girl who was mowing the yard. I would be discovered! My brother had no problem granting my request, of course, and I set out to do the chore.

In my mind, I was sure the unknown producer had my neighborhood on their scouting list and would decide to bet their career on the special little girl who was mowing her lawn. In reality, I did an awful job and it was way harder than it looked. Of course, no one who drove down our street stopped in awe of me. There was no Hollywood producer to discover me, no matter how unique and special I was.

Ahhh, the fantasy of discovery. I now know this to be a mental trick our brain uses when we want to avoid doing uncomfortable things. I see it in myself and my clients when we want a result and haven't yet been willing to be uncomfortable. We secretly (or not so secretly) want to be discovered — not only for our inner needs for significance, but also because we want a shortcut to glorious outcomes. Oprah isn't coming, y'all.

Perhaps it is human instinct to be efficient and use as little effort as possible. That's a nice story to tell ourselves around the discovery dilemma. It is much easier for us to want the world to make it easy, to have someone else validate us by betting on us, than it is for us to bet on ourselves — to take the risk, or put in the effort or pain to create an outcome we desire. It is easier to wish someone else would do the work for us. It is easier to ask others to refer our services and offerings to friends and family, to hope that we could go viral, or land an unbelievable opportunity that could skyrocket our trajectory.

We *want* the world to bet on us, we want the big return of a skyrocket, but we *need* to bet on ourselves. We need to be doing the daily and often boring or difficult work of becoming our own biggest fan and supporter. To be our fully expressed selves requires regular betting on ourselves. No one else's bet on us will be stronger.

These bets don't just have to be financial, although they can be. Betting on ourselves is an act of SELF-trust and belief. Our belief is the seed of power in all of our creations.

When our inner certitude feels stronger than our doubt — this is the moment we make the bet. We risk something (comfort, money, approval, time) in the present moment for the sake of the desired outcome of a future event. When we are willing to feel the discomfort of practicing something new, or repeating boring tasks, or investing in forward progress, we are making that bet on our deepest beliefs. When we choose authenticity in the midst of a world that wants us to conform, we are making that bet. Betting on yourself can feel like a big risk. Fear and doubt never go away, our excuses rise up regularly, and to bet on ourselves often looks like choosing wobbly certitude.

A core tenant of my success in life, work, and soul is being willing to bet on myself over and over, sometimes in small daily bets, and other times, in huge, bold double-down bets. Here are some of the bets I've made on myself, each not taken haphazardly, but carefully researched and considered. I bet on myself (over and over) by:

♡ Leaving the stable income of a salaried job to become a self-employed and 100 percent commission-based, and all-expenses-on-me small business owner.

♡ Investing money I didn't have to hire my first coach, so that I would be more likely to be a successful commission-based and all-expenses-on-me small business owner.

♡ Putting my marriage on the line for the sake of my authentic drive and expression — giving my husband an out if he ultimately wasn't comfortable being married to me without a salaried job. This was ALSO a bet on my marriage and I meant no disrespect by playing my partnership — one of the things I valued most — in my bet. It was a risk, for sure. Instead, I BELIEVED that my marriage would actually be better if I was able to be self-employed and pursue this career.

♡ Investing thirty thousand on an advertising campaign that ultimately failed. No ten times return like the ad gurus suggested. Yep, some bets fail. I may not have won in money, but I did win in education and lessons that I can now pass down to my clients.

♡ Hiring coaches, eating well, and doing boring daily habits.

♡ Being willing to make uncomfortable asks, by raising my fees from time to time, or by lowering my fees from time to time.

♡ Showing up as my authentic self, not just the polished leader, but also the leader in process.

♡ Hiring team members to do the things I am not good or efficient at doing, or that aren't a good use of my energy.

Betting on myself as a way of being and doing is better than the cash any angel investor could give me. For me, it is the ultimate self-accountability and one of the fuels of my success. When I bet on myself, I stand in the power of my belief, my possibility, and my resilience. I want this for you!

♡ What bets have you made on yourself?

♡ Are you betting on your successes or your doubts and excuses?

♡ Are you waiting for permission or are you willing to give yourself permission as a bet?

♡ Are you avoiding strategic risk or investment, and waiting to be discovered?

♡ What would you do if you really trusted yourself?

What would you do, or could you do, if you moved through and met discomfort instead of waiting for things to be easy and fun?

You can take bold moves in your life to be your own biggest fan and angel investor. Or, you can mow the yard, on your secret little street, and wait for Oprah to drive by. Discovery is just around the corner.

# Projection

I stood in the driveway of my eighty-year-old house in the West Oak Historic District of Denton, Texas. As my aging parents were loading up their car after a visit, I felt my worries about how my parents were living rise up, and I started a spat with my dad. The Crows, almost all of us, have an old crappy habit of engaging in the "You're doing it wrong" game with each other. And on this day, I found myself giving the same old speech again to my parents.

"You are living beyond your means. You have too much stuff. Who will pay for things when you are broke in your old age?"

There, behind the tailgate of my then-new truck, I caught myself. A tiny window of clear seeing opened up, and I saw the mirror in my words and allowed the truth to speak to me.

> *I* was living beyond my means.
> *I* had too much stuff.
> *I* could be headed toward broke.

Yes, I was concerned about my parents, and my someday self-appointed responsibility of liquidating an estate down the road. There I was again, over-functioning in their world and under-functioning in mine. I apologized to my dad and sent them on their way.

Within a week we had our giant, gorgeous, but on the edge of being a burden home under contract. Within three weeks we'd had a garage sale to get rid of years and years of collections and stuff we no longer needed (mostly mine). And within six weeks we'd downsized from three thousand square feet to eighteen hundred square feet, with mortgage payments about the same amount as the square footage.

Within a year, my husband and I both had our wills drawn up, powers of attorney, and medical directives assigned. I got additional life insurance, a disability policy, started maxing out my IRA, and finally started managing my money with "Profit First" so that I would have my taxes paid quarterly and with cash when due.

Holy shit that felt good.

Wanna lighten your load? Stop projecting onto everyone around you and clean up your own life. Everything shifts.

# Take Off the Spanx®

I once had an opportunity to "tell my story" on stage at an event with 250 people in the room. The story I chose to tell was of leaving corporate coaching and moving into my own version of a colorful, wild, and free me. I started out the talk in a sleek pencil skirt, high heels, and with my hair pulled back into a "professional twist." I was buttoned up, smoothed down, and I fit in with the image that was expected, hiding all my supposed flaws. As I told the story, though, I began to shed my outfit as a metaphor for shedding the personas that no longer served me.

After removing the outer layer of the fancy skirt and silky shirt, I stood there in my bra and underwear, covered only by my full cover-age-to-the-knee Spanx® shapewear contraption.

"What's left after I take all that off? THIS FUCKING GARMENT," and I did a short catwalk across the stage. Mind you, even with the Spanx®, it was not the size six me walking across that stage — it was the size fourteen me in a sausage casing, bulging in all the wrong places. The audience rolled with laughter and a bit of a gasp.

"This is meant to suck in everything and constrain me, so that you don't see that I am no longer a size four or six and 125 pounds at five-foot-ten, but that I am now 176 pounds."

I began to describe the sensations of wearing shapewear. I put my hands on my breasts, "My boobs are smashed. They are not even lifted, they're just flattened." The laughter in the room got even louder and I widened my eyes and grinned at the joy in the room and in my own ability to amuse a crowd with this glorious and often hidden truth.

The room clapped as if I were done, and I interrupted, "Oh, it gets worse . . ." I slid my hand down the center of my body down past my belly, "my crotch is sweaty. This is not what you see in Victoria's Fucking Secret . . . " with a pause for effect . . . "It's musty down there . . . because of THIS," I put my hands on the portion of the shapewear that covered my hips, "and my thighs are completely shoved together."

A woman in the fourth row tossed her head back and let out a boisterous laughing howl, "Buahooooo, hooooo, haaaauuuuu!" Smiling at the audience, I then offered, "If any gentlemen in the room want to try this on . . . " The women in the room erupted in cheers and applause.

Then I peeled off the body suit and stood there in my boring black and white cotton boy-short undies and a no-wire bra. For a moment or two, I stood there in the fullness of unclothed and unSpanxed me, holding the microphone with two hands and a sly smile.

"Cotton undies ladies, cotton! It's a miracle fabric. My boy-short underwear instead of those things that ride up your ass."

With my hands lovingly holding my boobs, I went on to describe the comfort of a no-wire, and completely comfortable bra, and then I slid my hands down to my soft, poochy belly. I reveled in what I thought of as "my extra thirty to forty pounds," or what I like to call my "happy fat." Here I remembered and told the stories of when, at thirty-seven, I still had my emaciated nineteen-year-old body.

At that time, I'd wake at 6:00 a.m., commute an hour to work where I would have thirteen to fifteen coaching calls a day, and then — to unwind — I would have a bottle of wine with friends at the office, followed by dinner, and then, more wine. After that, I would drive home and crash into bed. I described the insane pressure I felt to help my clients make money for our company through coaching and the continual criticism I received from the higher-ups about my personality — never my performance.

That season of my life was so stressful because I was living into the pressure and expectation of others, I was so fucking starved for acknowledgement, acceptance, and appreciation. I could feel my soul suffocating. And so, I left.

Trying to do all the things in an effort to be loved and approved of left me smothered. Just as I had done up on that stage, I began to strip down to my authentic self. I wish I could say it was sexy and fun, but it was awkward (just like removing that garment) and scary, and frustrating, and full of both self-doubt and an even deeper knowing that I had to figure out ME.

On that stage, and in life, I began a liberating process of discovering what I would do, wear, be, and believe if I was true to myself. After I stripped down to the cotton, I pulled on my favorite pair of jeans. The ones that make me stand tall. I pulled on a cotton baseball t-shirt, and I slipped on my black Converse® Chuck Taylor sneakers. I let down my twisted-up hair and released my natural wild curls. I opened up a few tubes of paint and I smeared my face with colorful marks.

On that stage I did something that so many want to do — I liberated myself from the expectation of traditional professionalism, of what a woman is supposed to be, and the mask she is supposed to wear. I made these deliberate and intentional moves with full knowledge of what I was letting go, in order to set me free.

# UnFiltered

"I would *never* have shared that."

The moment I heard those words, I *knew* I had to take the filter off as a leader. Early in my career as a coach — in my early thirties — I had the honor of being on a panel of "successful coaches" at a conference. It was a packed room, and I don't remember the question, I just remember my answer: "I have struggled with clinical depression for much of my life . . . and even as a beloved and successful coach, I still do."

There was an instant exhale in the room. After the meeting, I was getting a glass of water and when I turned around from the beverage table, there was a line of my colleagues waiting to talk to me. One by one, these beautiful, open hearts told me that they, too, struggled with depression, and they were so relieved and grateful I shared. My share — my voice — gave them hope and permission.

A few days later, I was sharing with my "boss" the deep connections and beauty of the coaches in our company. She saw no value in the connections and commonality, and she glared at me with disgust saying, "I would NEVER have shared that."

"Well, I did." I said calmly and walked out of the room with my heart and head held high. I was young and dumb in a lot of ways, but I knew — even then — that rising leaders needed *permission* to be human and that the expected perfection was suffocating us. I knew then that I would and could be someone who wasn't a victim of the struggles. I knew that I could be both human and powerful for those whom I mentored and led. I knew this was a possibility because it is what I needed, and I knew I wasn't alone.

Only once have I had a client tell me she didn't want to work with a coach who struggled with depression. I leaned in instead of backing away. I embraced her questions and her insecurities. We had a beautiful conversation about how I always shared hope, even amidst human struggles. Leaders have human struggles, too. And, we were here for something deeper than the facades of perfection. Sure enough, she struggled with depression herself, and instead of firing me at the end of that conversation, she dove in deeper.

I once had a client fire me via a long-ass projecting letter, because, in the context of a "behind-the-scenes" video for my clients, I had mentioned a spat I had with my husband. She said she didn't want a coach who argued with their spouse.

Let me pause while you laugh.

Right?

When I politely canceled her agreement, as she had asked, she then got mad that I didn't attempt to "handle her objection" and try to convince her to stay.

Gawd bless her.

I won't defend the human experience . . . I will share it. I am a woman of range, and you dear reader — leader or not — are a human of range. May you know that you are not alone. That there is no *negative* emotion, just uncomfortable ones that are shamed by society. No leader or teacher I ever had when I was young modeled BOTH/AND. I only ever saw the facade of perfection through the hollow hurting eyes of the people who rejected their own humanity for the same reasons I share mine. Ahhh . . . to be loved and cared for.

These days there are more transparent leaders, and I am grateful. Sure, it can be used as a weapon to manipulate or perform. Those people are just wanting to be loved and cared for, too.

> The more I love and care for myself, the easier and more relaxed I feel about sharing my underbelly with you.

For a recent wedding anniversary, my friend and client Brooke Genn took a few shots of my husband and me. He'd come out to an event I was hosting, and after a long day, I was not only exhausted, but sweaty, and certainly not dressed for photos. We happened to be in good light and Brooke wanted to grab a quick photo. The setting was beautiful, my energy high, and our love potent. Later, when I saw the photos, that is mostly what I saw — until my eyes dropped down to a left upper arm where my cellulite and flabby skin frumpled and dimpled, tempting me to reject everything else good in the photo that captured a delightful moment.

Old parts of me thought for a moment about having it touched up, and then, I let that thought go. What I see in that photo is a grown woman, who does have pocked-flabby-cellulite arms. It just IS. And it is a gorgeous photo. Arm and all, I see myself in all my perfect humanness, genuinely loving my man, and celebrating how in sixteen years we have grown so much together. The photo stands perfect as is.

There is no need for any of us to live an airbrushed life.

I love you. I love me.

Oh, happy day.

# The Gift of Coming Undone

Is it possible to be thankful for coming undone? For the unraveling and season of losing my shit over and over?

I'm a leader. A small, but still-public figure. My life's work is supported by being online, by being outspoken, by being visible, and by having a community. I've been complimented a thousand times for my light and positivity. There have been seasons I've lost my shit daily when I have felt more discomfort than joy. And, at times, I've certainly not behaved like the leader my early mentors taught me to be.

But I am not leading from a pulpit.

I am leading by *living my life* — feeling it all and choosing to look for love in all of it. I am being me.

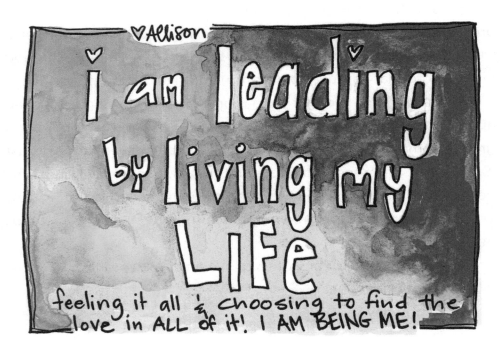

Coming undone is the scariest and most vulnerable experience I've had as a human. I've lost loved ones, and clients, and at times I even felt like I lost myself. But really, in losing my shit, in the coming undone, I'm finding more of myself.

I had both a beautiful, (truly — so much good) and frankly, crappy in a lot of ways, childhood. Trauma, alcoholism, chaos, raging, verbal abuse, and neglect set me up to be either a complete mess or a complete over-achieving control freak, to be a lover or a fighter. I armored up young. My first protective parts and coping parts were so terrified of the pain that they chose the rainbows and unicorns. They chose to fix things, to solve problems, to make peace. They chose to overcome versus succumb. They chose lemonade. They chose all these things because the rainbows and unicorns were palatable to the people around me.

At twenty-four I was clinically diagnosed with anxiety and depression. In my forties, I finally figured out why. I've pressed all these uncomfortable emotions down. I believed that if I let them out . . .

I would die from the pain.

People would leave me.

I would drag others down when I allowed those feelings to surface.

I would be seen as crazy and would subsequently be rejected.

I would be a mess and that is not ok.

I would not be the positive person I was supposed to be.

I wouldn't be able to choose love like I was supposed to.

I actually enjoy JOY. I enjoy seeing the glass half full. I enjoy feeling good. In the well over fifty thousand coaching calls I have experienced since I began this journey, I can safely say that every client has ultimately wanted one thing — to feel good. Every goal, achievement, desire, or healing was ultimately for the purpose of feeling good. Humans desire to FEEL good. We desire to avoid pain.

Over the years, I've had seasons of feeling "bad." September of 2015 was the beginning of one of my feeling "bad" seasons. Death of close loved ones, loss of stamina and physical health, deeper depression, tax burden, failures in business, parents aging and ailing physically and financially and me trying to *fix* it all. From the moment it all began to show up, I clearly saw that no coaching or spiritual bypass would work to stem the tsunami that was building. The only way out would be through. The ONLY way to healing and JOY would actually be to allow myself to feel all the feelings of coming undone.

They said I risked it all when I took off my clothes on stage as a metaphor for stripping down to my authentic self. But none of us knew that after getting naked, I'd have to turn inside out. And there I was, undone. And I wasn't ready to make nice or smoke unicorn and rainbow crack. Coming undone feels riskier than getting naked. Coming undone could topple my business. Coming undone could result in another husband leaving me. Coming undone could be the ultimate "too much" that could lead to friends leaving me as well.

That season, allowing in all the discomfort and pain became the work I could not NOT do. And my unfiltered self couldn't do it in private. I'd always shared behind the curtain, and so I shared the coming undone of that season, too. The political and global climate of that year, the election and the aftermath was my particular UNcorking. My Kraken was unleashed.

In that season I became overbearing, devoid of grace, and downright nasty and mean. I had had intentions of being curious and compassionate, fierce but loving, and instead I yelled and accused and raged. I sobbed and screamed and wept and was incapable or unwilling to listen. I felt ugly. I was terrified by the rage and fear and grief that clearly were and are alive INSIDE of me.

I haven't, and I'll bet most of you haven't either, been taught to feel these feelings in a healthy and appropriate way.

I. Am. Still. Learning.

I don't have answers. And today, despite the shame and guilt I feel, I also feel thankful. I am grateful that these hurting parts of me have demanded to be seen. It has not been pretty. And there is no quick making nice of it. And as my beloved Thich Nhat Hanh says,

> "There, there Anger, I see you. I will not leave you. I am here for you."

> "There, there, Terror and Fear, I see you. I will not leave you. I am here for you."

> "There, there, Pain I Think Will Kill Me, I see you. I will not leave you. I am here for you."

Finally, after twenty years of personal and spiritual seeking and practice, I finally see you. I will not leave you. I am here for you. And I am grateful for you. And somehow I know that I will be put back together again. And I will have many more undoings as long as I am human. And I will keep going.

This is an entirely new version of love. This is an entirely new creation and BEing of me. The story is not over. It is just beginning.

# Embrace the Quirky and Forget the Shiny Shit

Get the hell off the popular, everyone-is-doing-it train, please. There's a way that is expansive and helpful. There are also ways, usually sourced in comparison, that create constriction. Life and work aren't possible without the natural ebb and flow. There will be constriction.

I love when I recognize the constriction. I love it so much I want to clap, clap, clap for me, for recognizing it most of the time — not all the time, but most of the time. And when I recognize it, I remember: Allison, your head is a tool, your heart is the rule.

It's really easy to ignore what my heart wants. And my thinking parts like to say, "I've got this. I'm in charge, motherfuckers! Let's get this done, and everything will be okay."

When there is a problem to be solved, I often feel some underlying uncertainty. My protective parts can go into problem-solving mode, and this often involves disconnection from my body, my core SELF, and my heart. What I love is when I full-body remember what my SELF-led heart wants.

My SELF-led heart is quirky, original, and often senseless to anyone but me. Maybe your heart is, too. My heart, living in my body, remembers what works. My SELF-led heart knows that it can be fun, even when it's hard. My SELF-led heart knows how to use my head as the tool instead of letting thinking parts be the rule. Every once in a while, my head gets in there and rolls around, excessively, in strategy. When I lead with strategy, instead of letting strategy support me, I start to screw myself over. My quirky heart starts to get dehydrated and SELF gets smothered out by anxious and performing parts.

Do you ever do this? Do you ever think, "If I just have A in place, then B will happen?"

Really, I do love systems and structures — but, despite what all the Facebook ads for small business owners tell me right next to their "BUY NOW" buttons, systems and structures are there to support me, not lead me (even though sometimes I forget). They do not fuel me. They do allow my heart to rest at times with the support they provide, though. Systems can give me leverage, but my systems and structures need a little juice to function sustainably.

Sometimes, one's SELF-led heart needs to lock herself in the bedroom and rest and reset, or perhaps she needs an afternoon out on a blanket in the grass with a book and watercolors instead of spreadsheets and automations or plans. SELF-led hearts most assuredly require nourishing practices, rest, and lots of water, so as not to shrivel up and form cobwebs and resentment while being in this life. Nourishing practices, quirky creativity, deep belly breaths, and indulgent rest are, in fact, profitable business and life practices, even though the world wants you to buy their seven-point systems.

Inside of all your structure and all your systems and all your plans and all your visions and all your dreams lives your SELF-led heart. Your wild, tender heart, that desires companionship, camaraderie, collaboration, and connection. Sometimes I'm tempted by all the seductive and shiny stuff out there. Just like you, sometimes I don't even realize it's getting to me in a way that doesn't serve me. It hooks me. That's precisely when I need to remember to embrace the quirky and uniqueness of my own heart. Embrace what works for you, gentle reader.

What works for me is building relationships and connections (but not in-person-networking-extrovert-style-where-I-know-NO ONE. Hello mild panic). I like gentle, slow relationship-building through common experiences or through online content. What works for me is sharing my heart, showing my work, and connecting with one person, or with a small group. What works for me is speaking on stage in a connected and relational way. What works for me is writing and sharing. What works for me is substantial rest, unbridled expression, and daily creativity.

When I feel the pull of the shiny, when I get hooked by the mass messaging that tells me it's something OUTSIDE of me, I remember I have everything I need right here, right now. I surround myself with notes to remember to connect with my people and love on my people.

When I connect with me, and then I connect with my people, it all works and it feels good. For me, connecting with myself and connecting with humans is the answer. Why the fuck does everything have to be automated? Why are humans called "leads" in business? Gross. I don't need some slick opt-in or a mass of a few hundred thousand followers to convince you to work with me. I certainly don't need your mastery of the dark psychological arts and persuasive techniques (yes, there was an ad in my feed for a book and course on this last week). What if I just nurtured relationships in the direction of helping people with my heart and my expertise? What if I demonstrated my credibility, skills, and care as a human?

I've forgotten a hundred and one times. I've bought shiny shit I didn't need thinking it was the thing. Now, I KNOW the things that hook me. I know how to listen to my fears instead of buying shit for a quick fix. Not only do I focus on what I want and what my intentions are, I also am wisely aware of what I am not available for (contrary to what the Law of Attraction taught me). When scarcity and striving show up, instead of shoving them in the closet behind the heels I no longer wear and buying the most popular guru's online course because of that slick Instagram promotion, I now open my heart and my journal and listen to the fears and concerns. This resets my system and brings me back to SELF-led me.

When I first started out in real estate in 2003, the company I worked for had a program for new agents called Launch. Launch was a two-week immersive with classes in the morning and the afternoon. It was thick, intense, and exciting. Each class covered a different way to sell real estate. I think there was one contract class, one mindset class, and all the rest for the different ways that an agent could sell: open houses, cold calling, mass marketing, by referral, business to business, blah, blah, blah. When I started selling real estate in 2003, I dug in, desperately using my brain. And remember, my brain and thinking parts love to figure things out so that I can feel safe and certain, especially in new circumstances.

I was learning how to get clients, sell houses, be divorced, have my own business — all the things. I was tempted by the shiny, the mass glossy marketing, the perfect professional outfits, the ads in luxury neighborhood magazines, and driving a luxury car. My company promised all the systems and tools to make me successful, if I just "followed the model."

Bigger and bolder was better in that world. It was alluring, but I also felt constricted by it at times. A wise mentor back then told me, "Figure out what works for you." I knew I had to make this new life work for me, including my business. Failure was not an option.

How did I do it? By connecting with people. I used to have client parties. Not because I was great at throwing parties, but because with $250 left in my bank, a party was the best way to connect with the most people: in my own home, in an environment where I felt comfortable. I took my mess — my divorce, and the tiny sliver of cash left in my bank — and I solved the problem at hand! A "color party."

The first one was called The Fabulous Pink Party. It was around Christmas and I didn't want to get out my Christmas tree because I couldn't bear to get out all of the relationship ornaments from my now-failed marriage. I didn't want to feel sad. I was avoiding my feelings. I went to this store that we have in Austin called The Christmas Store, and I bought all pink ornaments as a giant FU to my ex-husband. The Fabulous Pink Party was born — everyone would wear pink, I served cheap food and pink drinks, and gave as favors, an epic mix-CD where all the songs had the word pink in them (you remember mixtapes, right?).

It was so fun. It was quirky, it was me — and it allowed me to love on my people! And eventually, my people referred me or chose me to represent them, even though they knew I was new.

You know what else worked for me? Selling houses to dates I met on Match.com, and smoking weed out of apple bongs on the lake with new friends . . . who eventually wanted to buy or sell a home. That wasn't in the Launch classes for new agents But it worked. It pissed the establishment leaders off, but it worked.

My quirky today is different from my quirky then. My quirky today is remembering that more is not better, and to always lead with my authentic heart. I do not need to spend more money, I do not need to have more systems.

What I know is that better creates more, naturally. Go love on your people. Master your skills, get really good at what you do, in the unique and specialized way you do it, and . . . did I mention love on your people? You most likely don't need a new strategy or a new ANYTHING. Could you create something new? Sure. And sometimes putting our heads down in creation takes us conveniently out of connection with others.

For now, remember what you LOVE about what you do and get back to you, then do what you *know* works. You don't need another thing to be successful. It's all working perfectly. More is not better, better is better.

I love you and I crave more of your authentic expression. Being in relationship and conversation with the REAL you is what matters. Relationships aren't systems to me . . . they are organic. As a Soul-Full and SELF-led business owner (and a human), my primary job is to remember that I'm a soul living a human life. I love the business stuff. I love the tools and systems and strategies, but without the soul and a SELF-led heart, it leaves me — and many of my clients and peers — shriveled and empty.

# I Am the Asshole

As we grow and begin to consider our true desires, character, and spirit in contrast to outer expectations, there are defining moments when we are presented with the option to choose our authentic selves or not. Moments, when we become aware that most always we've been choosing *they* and *should*, instead of ourselves.

To become our authentic selves, we have to first see, and then begin to move out of, our incessant people-pleasing and craving-for-approval ways. People-pleasing is seductive and delicious as we develop. *Everyone* wants to be liked and esteemed. The reward of people-pleasing creates muscle memory in our lizard brains — safe, secure, and rewarded for staying in the lines. In creating our lives in service of the esteem of others, we feel like we are kind, and we are often loved and accolated for our service and goodness, but in fact, we are quietly, and almost always subconsciously, needy and manipulative.

Hold the phone. Yep. I said it.

You, "kind and giving" one, taking care of everyone else, pleasing them — it feels good, eh? But are you really kind and serving? Or, possibly, are you, like I was, utterly and unconsciously manipulating and inauthentic because your lizard brain told you that if you didn't fit in and were rejected, you would DIE? This truth is often a gut punch to us people pleasers (it was for me), for we have convinced ourselves that we are good, giving, and kind. But are we?

Of course, we don't wake up and say, "I think today I will go manipulate someone into liking me so that I can feel loved." But we do go into the world with our own buckets empty and give everything else to others, then wonder why we are so empty at the end of the day. People pleasers are often, at the core, manipulating the opinions of others in order to be seen in a certain way. I dare say, as a recovering people pleaser, who often accused others of being assholes for not responding the way I'd hoped, that *I am*, in fact, the asshole. I am the one who gave my bent-and-compromised self as the holiest offering, expecting it to be always adored and worthy of love, all while hating myself for being so not me.

I am totally an asshole.

*(Dear Reader: calling myself, or YOU an asshole isn't mean! For me, it is ownership — and rather funny and liberating! Shout out to my client Joelle (shared with permission) for thinking her mother was such an asshole one day on a coaching call. In the end, she, and I, and all my clients watching realized, quite humorously, that WE'RE THE ASSHOLES. Now we proudly own it!)*

How are we able to even discover our true personality, spirit, or character when we are compromising and behaving so much for the approval of others? It took me years to see how subconsciously needy and manipulative I actually was as a grown woman. All my achievements and drive created a strong outer shell, and most of the world bought it. Hell, I believed it myself. I saw myself as smart, confident, capable, successful, productive, fun . . . all the things that I was in many ways. I was actually also building a strong and impenetrable facade around a deeply broken and insecure heart. A heart that just wanted to be acknowledged and appreciated. A heart that was terrified of being left, unloved, and un-adored.

There is a saying in the personal development world, "You can never get enough of what you don't need."

Yep. But I sure tried like hell.

# Emotions are NOT a Problem to Solve

So many of our uncomfortable emotions have been demonized. They are labeled as negative or sinful. We've been taught to:

- suck it up
- get over it
- kick fear's ass
- eliminate fear
- become fearless

- drive out fear with love
- give our fears to God
- and countless other ways to outsource the discomfort

Emotions aren't good or bad. Really, they aren't even negative or positive like traditional psychology labels them. They are comfortable or uncomfortable. They can be the source of behavior that can be helpful or harmful, but NO emotion is "bad" or "negative." Emotions have distinct and helpful information for us — but we haven't been taught to be curious or to listen to them, much less feel them.

We need our fears. We especially need the updated, validated, trusting versions of our fears. Fear is an important part of our biology and humanness. At times, fear can save your life. But we've been taught to overcome, outcast, banish, or purify our fears.

How's that working?

Spoiler alert: it's not. It's just outsourcing your authentic wisdom. It's obliterating your self-compassion.

Consider that fear is not your enemy. It is possible to befriend and get to know these uncomfortable parts. They have benevolent intent. At one point their behaviors protected you. Usually, they have some very valid, albeit, outdated concerns.

When we build a relationship — a partnership — with these parts, we can help them exist in our system in ways that are helpful and wise instead of reactive and harmful.

You were taught to rely on outside sources for validation and approval. You were taught (mostly unconsciously) to invalidate your own inner wisdom, even from emotions like fear.

Perfect Love doesn't cast out, reject, or exile Fear. Perfect Love listens to the concerns Fear has. Perfect Love holds presence for Fear without judging her stories. Perfect Love doesn't tell Fear how to be. Instead, Perfect Love asks Fear about her heart, her concerns, her stories, and the information she has to share.

"Hello Fear, I see you. I believe you. I am here for you."

Perfect Love befriends and builds trust with Fear, so that Fear can release its burdens and overly protective behaviors. Fear will still exist because it can't not exist. It just will serve a more updated and aligned purpose.

# Thinking Feelings Versus Feeling Feelings

Note the distinction.

The brain wants to think feelings.

Your body may or may not want to actually feel your feelings.

Because it can be unfuckingcomfortable.

But there is both a language of emotions and a sensation of emotions.

Wisdom is in the partnership of the two.

Note to self (and to you): Keep learning the sensations of your holy emotions.

Learn to speak with them, and even more,

Listen to the wisdom they share, both in body and thought.

# Curious Moves Toward

Again, for my Smartie++ people — we LOVE knowledge and learning, don't we? For me knowing things in my head gives me a strong sense of certainty and stability. Thinking can be both a liberation and a delight for me. Ideas are like candy at times. Other times, thinking is my bondage, like getting full-body-stuck in a tangled ball of twine looping over and over again.

My thinking parts think they have most of the answers. Of course they do! They work diligently to keep me from slowing down and going deeper. They prefer my energy in my head, because all of my old wounds and terrified Exiles live down in my body, buried, hidden in my tensions, at the back and bottom of my heart. In my body they have a subconscious memory — nothing cognitive is required to wake them and shake them into a frenzied terror of remembering.

I see this in my clients too, the spinning we all do in our heads, creating a bigger and bigger gap between our thinking and our deepest truths. Sometimes my thoughts remind me of a ceiling fan blade spinning. I stick my hand up to grab a blade and stop the motor. Like when I was a child playing the game of "stop the fan," there is a slight trepidation in sticking my hand into this whirling machine, but there is a knowing that I'll be just fine — a slight sting and then everything stops while the motor burns on.

I interrupt the whirling thoughts, not because I'm rude or impatient, but because to really connect we have to stop the process and move toward that which we fear. When our nervous system feels a threat, we will fight, flee, freeze, fawn, or froth (dramatic over thinking). This is our biology. Our conditioning also trained us to suppress, outsource, bypass, and avoid. All of that is only a momentary relief.

To navigate and soothe these pains inside, we have to learn the skills of moving toward these parts of us that are hurting. How do we do that? We become curious. Curious with more than our minds. Curious with our breath, and body, and our full presence.

I was taught "the skill" of curiosity as a series of coaching questions. Smart and sterile questions that were meant to uncover the deepest mindset blocks in my clients and myself. These questions promised to find the one misaligned belief deep within. When that belief was uncovered, watch out — with that corrected misaligned belief I could be back on my way to productivity and success (and so could my clients). You know, "change your thinking, change your life."

I was taught awareness and noticing solved 98% of my problems. And for a long time, awareness and noticing served me, but not completely. To be only an observer, to be only aware, left my innermost parts still craving more. Awareness and noticing kept me separate from these tender parts, but these parts simply needed my full presence and attention.

Curious questions and awareness — all from my head — left my head HUGE and every other part of me dehydrated and starved. Same with my clients. A common frustration for me and my clients was, "I *know* this in my mind, I *know* what to do, but part of me ends up resisting, or procrastinating, and not doing it!" This is followed by shame, and self-judgment, and guilt, and then, we are even further from our desires and goals.

For years I was taught (and taught and taught) that this was a "mindset issue." I was wrong and so were the "gurus" that espoused this knowledge. If it was as easy as changing our minds, as easy as a decision, those of us who struggle with these polarizing thoughts and behaviors would have handled all that by now. It isn't a light switch decision of the mind. It requires a curious and compassionate journey down into the body. And like any new adventure, when I first started this journey, everything was an awkward mystery. I just KNEW I had to move toward my own depths.

Bringing all of my breath and body and presence to my curiosity allowed me to move toward those starved, aching, ailing parts — slowly and gently, and with compassion. The head was not made to hold all of us. But our hearts and our bodies, they are miracles that can support us if we will turn toward ourselves. My heart and miraculous body can hold it all, and so can yours.

These are learned skills, so be gracious with yourself. Start slow, ask for help if it feels strange. Often it does for me. Being held by my coaches and therapists and friends who know how to help me stay connected to me is part of the process. It helps me build these skills over time.

If you aren't ready to move toward those parts that feel parched, perhaps just start with not running away. In my head, I notice the cravings and urges — to flee, to fight, to shop, to squirm, to drink, to escape, to avoid. Hello craving and urges — I see you. I'm here for you. I will not leave you. It's a beautiful and helpful start to notice and then breathe. Be still and breathe slowly, gently, until you feel even a bit of release.

You are not alone.

UNARMORED

There are so many of us new to this. So many of us are willing to learn because we must, because the incessant disconnection from SELF is no longer sustainable. And because there is hope in remembering and reconnecting with who we really are.

PART 6

# Compared In the Womb

Hello, Ms. Crow. Here is an ultrasound of your baby. You are only in the first trimester, and yet, already, for your benefit and for the benefit of the baby, we have measured and estimated your baby's size and started measuring her against all the other baby sizes ever in existence.

We've given her a numeric representation called her *percentile*. This number will tell you that she is either perfect or imperfect, or somewhere on the sliding scale of 1 to 100. No matter what her number, you will feel either a mild or extreme anxiety about that number.

Oh, and as soon as you give birth to this child, we will snatch her from your bosom to measure her head and length, and weigh her before she even seemingly starts to breathe. Again, we will jot in our charts a numeric percentile and those measurements.

And again, you will feel some strong emotion about these assessed values, and while you look her lovingly in the eye as you breastfeed, or as you give her a bottle of formula, you will quietly (inside your heart) panic that your child is okay, or maybe she isn't. Then you will anxiously overthink about how, even *if* she is ok now, you are most certainly going to fuck up your child, and both you and she will be horrible forever because of it.

With each visit to our office, we will continue to measure and compare, and as you follow along in all the expert books, you will also continue to measure and compare. Everyone will be measuring and comparing everything about this baby until she isn't a baby anymore. Then, when she is a child ready for school, the measuring

and comparing will all continue, both in the home and in the institu-
tions, and yes, still at the doctor's office, all, of course, for *her benefit*.

For the rest of her life, she will be measured and compared, cat-
egorized, and labeled, and grouped and assigned, so that she will
eventually only know herself in comparison to both others and the
status quo of the system, culture, and micro-culture, current media
and trends, and of course, strong opinions of others, to which she is
exposed.

Out of breath yet? Me, too. And that is the short version.

# The War Between People-Pleasing and Fuck You

Anger and I have had a life-long relationship. I grew up in a house where anger was ever present, lurking even in calm and loving moments, ready to erupt at random. So much anger and verbal violence. Even though there was also love and affection, I knew that Anger could pop up and threaten me, my siblings, or my mother at any time. Anger could, and often did, explode, even when friends were over or when we were in public places. It wasn't just confined to the secrets of our home. Anger also came with her sidekick, Humiliation. While my dad introduced me to Anger, I introduced myself to Humiliation.

As a child, my body never could fully relax and I found myself "anxiously on guard" as my primary state. Creating a 360 degree view as a protective device, my little Inner Being formed into one who shrank and bent to avoid Anger, especially in personal relationships. Being anxiously aware also developed parts of me that had a strong intuition, emotional empathy, and a proactive assertiveness. My nervous system attuned itself to perceive even the slightest threat. These parts protected and served me in society as a student, as a young leader, and even as a young woman. Leadership and achievement, lauded by the masses, often hide the trauma of our youth. Is it intuition — some special gift from the gods — or is it just an adaptation to trauma?

For many years, my compliant parts and leadership parts fiercely protected the buried and tender parts of me, but as my bones grew, so did my Anger. It wasn't just my father's anymore. I became the one with hidden, unexpected explosive heat. While my father's was almost daily, mine was mostly buried deep inside until something hit it, like a tripwire, and like a giant, hot, flash, it flared and flooded me. This amiable, outgoing woman, who genuinely had a caring and benevolent heart, would become Rage and Verbal Attack, usually on people I deeply loved.

The power struggles in the early years of my current marriage were the first to help me see what was happening under the surface when I would get so reactive and angry. In conflicts with loved ones, I could see clearly that my strong reactions were almost always related to my fears of being unloved and left. When Anger and her hot flashes even peeked into my experience, I began to drop in and search for, and tend to my fears. At the time, I didn't have the language of parts, but my relationship to myself began to shift. I saw that beneath my Anger was Fear, and now that I knew she was there, I could tend to her. I no longer needed the protection of my Anger. For years, she was soft and silent, and rested . . . Until the morning TFG (The Former Guy) was elected.

Anger woke up with me on that November election morning and became my teacher for the next four years (who am I kidding, in the current political climate, Anger is still teaching me). No longer could positivity and spiritually mask all the emotions I'd buried deep inside. I got swept up in the divisiveness of the political and racial climate. My opinions and judgment were stronger than my peace.

Anger began to frighten me when she showed up with Hate. They shoved the people-pleasing parts away with fearful shame. They brought in the Fuck You parts — a strong and violent mob of older inner-teenagers. This cluster of parts grabs their weapons of words, they shake their fists, and yell at the news and my Twitter feed. Some of these parts wish they could actually use a knife and inflict legitimate harm. These parts would rather cut someone to bits or smash heads in than let me feel that pain again.

What, too violent? But there are violent parts in me. These parts front with their "fuck you" and "I will kick their ass," but mostly only from the safety of my own mind, because that anger and violence — of course — is not acceptable. Occasionally my "fuck you" parts do sneak out and respond to tweets, and then another part of me deletes the response before I can push post. Still, another anxious part wonders if the FBI or CIA is watching the nasty things I say to awful Texas politicians.

These parts showing up, with the unfiltered hatred scared me. The mental and emotional war between all of these polarized parts horrified me. I found myself feeling full-body hatred for people I'd loved my whole life. I found myself uncertain, and no amount of knowledge could ease what was hurting inside me. I knew I had the choice to quit "caring," but that wasn't an option for my soul. I began to curiously U-turn my judgment and hatred inside, and finally, I reached out to a trauma-informed leadership coach and therapist. She introduced me to my now beloved Internal Family Systems and the lens that allows me to see my parts, my pains, and mySELF.

Once I put on the lens of IFS, literally EVERYTHING in my inner and outer world looked different. It felt different. No circumstantial change occurred, but by being willing to connect and be curious with Anger, and with Hatred, and even with my desire to PUNCH EVERYONE IN THE FACE, I began to see how my "parts" were protecting me from pain.

Just like during the arguments with my husband, underneath the protection of Anger was Fear, and Sad, Sad, Sadness. Inside was the saddest and most frightened little girl, the girl that worried about everyone else: The girl who tried to manage her family's emotions, but couldn't; the girl who was terrified of disagreement and conflict; the girl who desperately wanted to have an open heart but dreaded the pain of rejection; the girl that felt excruciatingly alone and awkward; the girl that needed to be cared for.

I could see that underneath my Anger about politics, was really a deep care and concern for humanity, and the way we treat each other, and the laws and legislation that affect us all, especially marginalized people. Caring too much hurts, and not caring isn't an option for me and my inner family. But what would stop the war inside?

Through that IFS lens, and upon the advice of my therapist, I became willing to no longer *fix* these parts. I just called in Calm and began to connect and listen.

I've been listening, and through listening, compassion, and curiosity, I am able to witness and to understand. And when I do, the little me inside and her protective parts release layers of the burdens she has carried for a lifetime. She softens, she opens, she rests. As a wise woman once said, the more I meet all the parts of me, the less I want to punch other people in the face. At fifty, Anger still sits on the surface of my being, but she is welcomed and not feared. We are building a trusting relationship, and she is certainly not exiled away.

I am finding ways to let Anger and Fuck You be heard. I am finding ways to let my Bleeding Heart parts be held without turning completely away. And as we here in America approach another election season, I am deep in the practice of meeting these parts, over and over, gently, gently, gently.

# Life Is about Becoming Human

You are a thoughtful being living a human life, and so, from one human to another, I just want to acknowledge this truth. You are HUMAN.

I'm tired of spending life trying so fucking hard to NOT be human. It's exhausting.

Being human is messy. As humans, we crave love and security and belonging. It's not about eliminating your doubts and fears. It's about *leading* your doubts and fears. Trust your human self.

Your humanness is holy.

Just for one moment.

You don't need the validation you think you need.

You don't need the confidence you think you need.

You don't need the worthiness or enoughness you think you need.

You definitely don't need the "how to" you think you need.

You don't need to gather all the information you think you need.

You *do* need to put down the drama.

Decide. Choose. And take one step.

# Depression

I want to be the coach and leader that is happy and joyful, and I am. I am also a coach that has had a lifelong struggle with depression and anxiety. It's been a long time since I've been hit with what I call a "flatline," and yet, here it comes, pecking its way to the surface. I don't want it here. I want to be creating and writing and enjoying my friends and family. I want to be making art, and playing, and cooking. I do not want "flatline" here. But it is here, and it has glorious information for me.

I have a few ways I support myself when these flatline emotions show up. I no longer press them down. I get scared and fearful sometimes, that my people won't love me if I'm so flat. I tend to isolate at times, and even with that tendency, I'm sharing the truth because that's what I came here to do.

I'm listening to the wisdom of this clog of parts and emotions. I can already feel and witness a layer of grief — a really deep and personal loss. It's time to feel it. I notice the sensations of tightness in my chest and across my back. I acknowledge and validate in my own mind, to the grieving part of me, "Of course this loss hurts, you cared so deeply, and you had hopes that were disappointed. I see you Grief, you are welcome here. I won't leave you." I breathe a deep compassionate breath, and I hear Grief tell me it will allow me to open up my heart even more . . . To myself, to my loves, to you.

I am here to swing wide. To feel it all, to be divinely HUMAN. The joy is nice, but to heal, we must go to the underworld. I'm here to joy and to heal. I share to normalize, because I know it's so much easier to hide in silence.

What helped when I felt really flatlined recently:

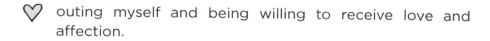 outing myself and being willing to receive love and affection.

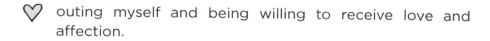 deep connection with a friend who was also struggling. Struggling together and just being compassionate with one another was uplifting for us both.

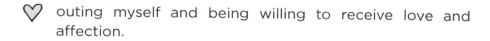 moving my body — allowing the grief to stomp on the ground during my walk and letting myself cry and acknowledge feelings.

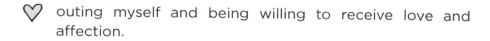 not positivity bypassing.

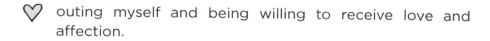 sharing with my besties — conscious complaining.

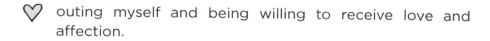 remembering that depression has information for me. I found the information that needed my attention and witness.

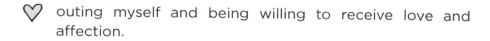 lots of water and all my vitamins and meds.

 lunch and connection with my husband and dear friend.

Instead of crawling in bed, I got some behind-the-scenes work done. It took a lot longer than I anticipated, and cussing at the computer seemed to discharge the last bit of stale energy. I felt accomplished by taking gentle action, and, wow! The computer didn't even get its feelings hurt.

I am Loving you, here from the ebb, knowing the ebb has wisdom and the flow always comes back.

# Don't Coach Your Parts

I am about to share with you one of the best, most important things that my very first IFS coach and therapist shared with me on our second session, almost in passing, and it changed *everything* for me. My very first exposure to IFS was with leadership coach and level three IFS practitioner therapist, Rebecca Ching. On our second call, she said in passing, "Oh, by the way, don't coach your parts." I can now translate that to "don't *parent* your parts" and "don't *teach* your parts."

Here's why this is so valuable: Being a coach and being in personal development, I'm prone to be a fixer. I'm prone to be a let's-solve-the-problem-and-get-it-all-better-right-now person — maybe you are, too. I also have a certification in parts work modality that involves parenting your inner child.

In IFS, there is a distinction between caretaking parts and self energy, capital S E L F. There is a presence and acclamation with SELF-energy that is so powerful for managing the parts that try to control and fix everything. Many of our caretaking parts are trying to manage and control, so that you won't feel pain. Their primary goal is to create a life where you never hurt again, so that you never feel that pain again. These caretaking parts are very skilled.

A couple of fundamentals of IFS and internal parts work with self energy are that: 1) all parts are benevolent; and 2) all parts are welcome. None of your parts are getting fired. We just want to help them upgrade, update, or step into more alignment with the present. Those of us in the coaching industry work with a lot of managers in the internal system. (Brief primer reminder: We all harbor within us managers and firefighters, a core SELF, and exiles who are our deepest inner wounded parts.) Managers and firefighters are the protective parts of us that are keeping us from tapping into the pain of exiles. I have a full cohort of caretaking parts — I call them my parenting and coaching parts, because they really like to fix things. I have noticed that many of my clients in the coaching realm are very good at solving problems — in fact, they are paid to solve problems, so that's what they tend to fall into with themselves, too!

These protective parts and exiles don't want to be fixed, though, and trying to fix or coach them sends them even further into protective mode. What these parts need, instead of fixing or coaching, is presence, witness, and curiosity. These inner caretaking and coaching parts need calm presence and an attunement to SELF, but they don't know how to say that. So, when you're doing this work and can tap into self energy, that calm, clear, connected, compassionate energy, and when you begin to find and feel your parts, you have to allow space to slow the process down. Allow yourself and your parts to attune energetically and physically for a moment, without words.

My system needs calm and connection before it can get to anything else. Your parenting, coaching, and caretaking parts probably also need a little bit of your compassionate calm, presence, and then curiosity. Instead of you telling your parts how things are going to be, simply begin asking and witnessing. Tell me more. What is it you'd like me to know? I'm here for you. I won't leave you. I see you. I'm listening. Let them talk.

So often we have been taught to shut up or shut down our inner critic. But what if you said instead, "Oh, hello, inner critic, I see you. I'm here for you. I'm listening." And with your breath and your intention, and all of your somatic awareness, you create presence and compassion with this part. And then, what you'll find after presence and compassion, is curiosity. "I see you're here. Now, how come you showed up right now? What would you like to share with me? How may I build trust with you? What are you afraid of? How are you protecting me?"

Listen.

# Addicted

We are addicted to the doing and the timelines. But y'all, the timelines are all fucking artificial.

I can't tell you how to do your life and your business when extra-extra comes up. But I can lovingly and powerfully remind you that — yes, you, human — you do not have to be supernatural or have supernatural powers. I know there are parts of you that love supernatural powers, but you can — as a human being — decide what you can control and what you can't control. And from those things that you can and can't control, you can also decide what you're willing to set aside for a while.

Let's engage some curiosity to get clarity: What's important and urgent? What's important and not urgent? What's urgent and not important? And what is not urgent and not important? Here's the fun part: what's not urgent and what's not important, immediately comes off your list.

What do you really need to do? What are you making up in your mind that you have to do?

I'm the boss of me. You are the boss of you. Your energetic resources are important and needed elsewhere.

# Slow Is Fast

Y'all love to read the slow down and rest memes on social media, but what happens if you do it? It's itchy, it's confronting. It's uncomfortable. Parts of you will freak the fuck out. And this is where the gold is. You can't build self-trust by avoiding parts of yourself. You can't hear yourself if you fill the room with noise and refuse to listen.

Business owners, I'm talking to you, especially. The grind and hustle culture has sucked you in. I KNOW your heart is in your business. What is happening to the cells in your body, though? How are you avoiding YOU? What are you shoving aside that longs for your loving presence? Is it possible to be slow and successful? Your nervous system may prefer the drama, but what if?

What if slow could give you flow? What if slow and present were the path to self-trust?

What if you COULD be with all these itchy parts of you? What if they were soothed by your calm and connected presence? What if slow was the fastest path to your becoming all that you desire?

# Even Slower than That

Against all other urges, she allowed herself to go slow.

The Drivers inside began to worry that the business would fall apart.

They told her she would be behind and scolded her for not growing.

Something inside whispered, "I am growing — here — doing nothing but breathing and being me."

Something inside knew she would trust herself to be where she was — to be only right-here-now.

She met with existing clients and journaled.

She had deep conversations and listened to books.

She also slept, and slept, and slept.

She sat in the swing and let it hold her like a womb.

She let the sun shine on her face, even without sunscreen, and she watched the hummingbirds play and the cardinals feast.

And her nervous system began to heal. Slowly. Slowly. Slowly.

No — even slower than that.

And it was good.

# Slow Tango

My husband, since the day I met him in my mid-thirties, has been telling me to slow down. "Slow down, Allison. Slow down, slow down, slooooowwwww down."

I'm a fast mover. My brain thinks fast, I historically get shit done, and I can make decisions in a split second. I am fast, fast, fast. This fastness served me well, until it didn't. In my mid-forties, my body changed and begged for a more gentle pace. I could feel my soul's call to slow down. Slowing down was awkward at first. The muscles have a memory, and even if I slowed my body down, my mind raced with anxiety about all the things I *should* be doing, about how much more I *should* be producing financially. Slow took practice, and when my body started showing signs of illness that required massive rest, I was forced to slow down. It felt like failure . . . Until . . . Until I heard *the song*.

Before I tell you about *the song*, let me disclose — music and dance are not my primary languages (to the dismay of my husband). Rhythm has always been a mystery to me. I enjoy some music, and when I do feel it, I feel it deeply.

Eighties music always gets me to smile, and it really is the only music that calls me irresistibly to the dance floor. Like most anyone, certain songs call forth emotional memories from my past. I feel like I was conceived to Willie Nelson because when I hear his music my bones vibrate and I experience a deep sense of my roots. Depeche Mode brings me back to my melancholy lovesick days in junior high. Madonna was my first concert, and in college, I had a brief love affair with nineties country music. It feels like a small, narrow musical experience when I compare myself to others who seem to speak the language of music often. Yet, these few genres have been my musical notes. Anything beyond my personal basics and experience rarely moved me until I saw and heard a slow tango.

A few years ago, a friend of mine shared a video on Facebook of her doing the tango with a partner. As I clicked the little white "play arrow," I was surprised to see and hear a tango; not a spicy, fast, and racing tango like the ones I was familiar with, but a slow, gentle — while still structured — tango with a tempo that seemed to give me a sense of knowing and groundedness. The song was *Snow Prelude N2* by Ludovico Einaudi. (Please go find it on Spotify now and listen as you read.) Seeing this dance and hearing this song gave me the gift of *feeling* into a new rhythm and pace that were never before possible for me.

My soul said to me, "THIS. IS. YOUR. PACE."

"What pace is your Soul calling you to go."

In my mind's eye, the chaos of the world, while still existing, could swirl around me in all its frenzy — but I could drop in and my breath and being could do this pace to perfection. Everything that I had been doing at this fast, grinding, and striving rhythm could also be accomplished at this slow tango pace.

Have you seen those videos, where someone is color blind, but they put on new glasses that correct their vision — or when a child, who is deaf, receives a hearing implant and then can hear her momma or daddy for the first time? This tempo felt like these moments to me — a whole new possibility for my being.

I could breathe. Before, I was doing all the things (and don't get me wrong, I had some fun), but I often felt thirsty and dehydrated with the pace I believed the world needed from me. I had always felt such urgency. An urgency to live and create in a certain way. A pressure to respond, to perform, to hurry, to next, next, next.

Slow Tango gives me space to enjoy my creations, space to process my thoughts, and space to pay attention to my inner world. Slow Tango gives me the rest and recovery which are actually necessary for exquisite performance; my own personal metronome — gently setting the pace for a new, more aligned way of being. And, in the spaces between moves, with each breath, my nervous system began to heal.

Slow Tango has now been my way of being and moving for more than five years. Less really *can* be more, and better, really is better, and slower gets me where I am going right on time.

# I Am Me

We can begin again at any moment. We can remember everything true and loving about ourselves. We can reduce the noise that doesn't support us. We can come back to center. We can breathe and be in the present moment. We can call back our loving intention — not for what will happen, we can't always control that — but for the WHO we intend to BE with ourselves when the world around us goes to shit.

> I will be connected to ME.
> I will be calm.
> I am calm.
> I am compassionate.
> I am present.
> I am breath for me, I am here in this body.
> I am ME.

# Goals

If your goals are attached to your enoughness,

    your excruciating need to be liked,

    or to finally feeling lovable,

    or to finally feeling worthy. . .

    then NO achievement can ever satisfy you for more than the brief dopamine hit.

    And, any misstep or failure along the way will crush you.

# Permission to Wander

Is direction really needed to achieve? Is achievement really needed to thrive? Perhaps there is a place between where one could wander from here and create, to there and create, and then to bed to rest, and then get up again and wander all over in completely new ways.

I once wandered across London. Technically I had a direction and a place to be by a certain time. But I left with hours to spare and a map that led me in a general direction. It turned out to be a four-hour walk — this way and that. Seeing things that I could never have seen had I taken a cab or rideshare. Feeling my feet on the sidewalks and taking the time to touch the edges of buildings that were more ancient than anything in my home country, crossing little alleys, and discovering miniature parks and gardens.

What I remember is not the things I saw, but simply, giving myself the permission for it to take time. Permission to NOT be so efficient and direct. I wandered, alone, to this big park where a hundred other people were supposed to meet. I opted out of all the meet-and-greet games and watched from my spot on the grass, soaking in the earth of a London park, and peacefully watching colleagues, friends, and strangers play those dumb connection games at the start of conferences. It was delightful.

Then when it was over, I joined up with a small group of souls I adored. We chose to wander the way home on foot, laughing, lingering, a sort-of-line of us meandering down various paths. I'm not sure who knew where we were going, because it really did seem so far from our home base hotel. But eventually, this gaggle of friends found their way to a pub and had things Americans and

Canadians have in London pubs, and our wandering continued in our conversations.

Wandering is an essence and energy I quite like. I think I shall be more intentional about wandering more often. (If that isn't too much of an oxymoron.) I will delight in my wanderings — intentional or not.

# Crossing Over

There is this before, and then this crossing over the threshold, before the coming home to yourself. To MY coming home. I notice my words are big and loose and spacious and that is the life I want to live.

Big and loose and spacious, but within the clear boundaries of what I am available for, and what I am not.

The threshold from other-focused, or parts-led and fully armored-up protecting all my old wounds at all costs, to coming home to SELF. This journey of taking the space to meet so many of the parts of me that I used to despise and fear, to be present and connected with these parts, and to gently learn to create that space for SELF to become the center and leader of me. This passing seems to be a bit brackish. There is an acclimatization required of body, mind, and presence — similar to the places where salt and freshwater meet.

> And then . . .
> after some time in the discomfort . . .
> everything becomes clear, and I am home in the freshwater of ME.

# Heal Here:
# A Door to the Underworld
# (The Way Out Is Through)

A prayer for difficult emotions:

Make room for your holy sadness.

Make room for your benevolent, frantic anxiety.

Make space for your sacred, aching grief.

Allow the presence with the pain of your burning anger.

Be intentional with this.

Master presence with these, and they will not master you.

When you reject these holy parts of you (as most society has taught you to do) . . . you are rejecting your own self.

When you shun these away, or press them down . . . well, you already know how they erupt and dis-ease you.

Courage rests between Self-trust and your willingness to be uncomfortable.

PART 7

# Courage

# BE Feelings

*"Stop that crying bull shit."*
*"Suck it up and put on a brave face."*
*"Smile, pretty girls look better with a smile."*
*"Get your shit together."*
*"You are out of control."*
*"Anger is unbecoming."*
*"Stop being so emotional."*
*"You are crazy."*
*"Are you on your period?"*
*"Man up."*
*"You worry too much."*

What was said to you? What were you taught from an early age about strong emotions, especially the so-called negative ones? For me, it was both the cultural and societal pressure to suppress strong emotion, and my father's repeated strong and threatening reactions. From an early age, strong and visible emotions seemed to be an indicator that I was somehow misbehaving, unhinged, or irrational. I can remember being a young teenager in the middle of emotions and tears, and my dad, in his tall, intimidating frame, barking at me from his own trauma to "STOP THAT CRYING BULLSHIT." In a horrified gasp, my little teen lip would quiver in fear and confusion, and I would do my best to suck the tears back and stop the flow of feelings.

I didn't know how to *not* feel — it was just coming up in me and felt so natural, but my father, and many of the men in my life, always seemed to be so bothered by my emotions. My father would get emotionally or physically aggressive, a verbal jab, a hand raised, a look of disgust and displeasure. That little girl learned how to press down feelings to be safe, to be loved, pleasing until she became a young woman of nineteen who struggled with clinical depression, just like her father, and her grandfather before her.

In my early thirties, I remember my then five-month-old niece crying in a playpen in my parent's backyard. My dad and I were standing close by, and as her tears turned to screams, once again, he erupted — to a five-month-old baby — "Stop that crying bullshit!"

I scooped up my niece and put myself between her and my father, and I looked over my shoulders with the most piercing glare, and through gritted teeth, I rebuked him, "NEVER say those words again."

I didn't have to explain more. My dad, who to his credit, has been doing his own inner work for many years, heard me. I could see in his softening eyes that he recognized not only the absurdity of telling a baby not to cry, but that also he had done damage to his own child, now an adult standing before him.

That was the beginning of a reclamation for me. At that moment I could see the blueprint — on his life and mine — of not being able to FEEL. I could clearly see how all the pressing down in his own life had been projected on us, and how I had done the very same thing to myself and others. I would not let that happen to my innocent nieces, and I would course-correct and lead, from SELF, the parts of me who did the same.

It was about that age that I began professionally pursuing personal development, and it would be another ten years before I began to learn to notice, to actually feel and process strong, difficult emotions. Since that day, I've never heard my father say those words again.

And even if he does, what I will say to myself and to you is:

"I see your tears, small sniffles, and big snotty sobs. All are welcome here, I believe you, and it is good to feel through your body."

# BE Too Much

In thousands and thousands and thousands of coaching calls I've experienced in my career, almost every single client taps into a sense of insecurity and not-enoughness. And what I've seen is that the SPIRIT within is begging for her (or his) too-muchness to be set free.

You *are* too much.

Too loud. Too quiet. Too straight. Too wild. Too shy. Too skinny. Too fat. Too confident. Too insecure. Too smart. Too dumb. Too emotional. Too expressive. Too aggressive. Too sexual. Too demure. Too safe. Too risky. Too conservative. Too woo-woo. Too crazy. Too talkative. Too insane. Too much.

I don't think we doubt our worth and enoughness. I think we doubt our too-muchness.

TOO MUCH WOMAN — I celebrate you. I am asking you to be your TOO MUCH SELF.

What if you embraced and loved all of your too-muchness? What if you allowed her to be expressed and embodied in every moment? You don't have to shrink to control people's opinions of you. The antidote is giving yourself validation and permission to live into all of your too-muchness. There in that space, you will find the love and acceptance you craved all along, all there inside your own TOO MUCH heart.

# Be Your Truth

Dig.
Dig deep.
Deeper still.
Beneath the voices,
Toss aside the oracle cards,
The books, the classes,
The teachers, and leaders.

Look and listen deep into your soul.
Beneath all the protective parts.

If you look — really look —
And listen — really listen -
You will find the place where the light is sourced.

What does your soul KNOW that is your truth?

# BE Human . . . The Most Spiritual Thing You Can Be

I spent so many years bypassing my beautiful and wonder-FULL humanness. You don't have to leave yourself. You don't have to press her down or exile her to the darkness or even try to transmute her through meditation. Instead, what if we allowed ourselves to BE compassionate and connected? What if we listen? Be there for yourself. You are worthy of it.

I wish BEING YOURSELF was as easy as flipping a switch. If only it was as easy as saying or making a simple decision. The truth is . . . We don't KNOW ourselves completely. We are taught from birth to annihilate and exile parts of ourselves. We are taught to judge and shame and bypass and hide and mask parts of ourselves.

Over and over clients bring up parts of themselves they seem to have so much shame around, parts they shove away and try to escape; parts like overthinking, procrastination, insecurities, perfectionism, and fears. All this shoving and hiding and self-shaming takes energy and leaves us exhausted — our parts are exhausted, and ignoring only makes them bigger.

You know this. I know this. So what do we actually do?

Just like we learned shame and judgment, we can learn to meet and BE with all of our parts. Not to coach them, or fix them, or even send them to the light.

Seriously. Fuck off with your positivity and light at all costs shit. Fuck off with the obligation to be happy, to smile, to cheer up, to stop complaining. We have got to be more welcoming to all parts of ourselves.

Learning to meet and BE present, connected, and compassionate with our most hidden parts is — frankly — a new relationship and requires new skills.

You can't have wholeness while dismissing some of the parts, but you've been taught to fear them. What if they have wisdom for you? What if you actually knew how to BE with your grief, or sadness, or rage, or shame, or your too much part, or your not enough parts?

Just typing this brings physical peace to my whole mind/body.

Get to know all of your parts. Get to know your internal family. Get to actually know yourSELF.

# BE Embodied

I have friends and colleagues who live and breathe embodiment. They are comfortably free to dance and move and breathe and eye-gaze and pulse their entire beings in public. It's natural and pleasing to them. As I've mentioned before It freaks me the fuck out.

I've been in a handful of aerobics, yoga, or step classes where the instructor made fun of my awkward movements. I remember one step class in my twenties. The instructor found me (even though I was hiding in the back row) — my rhythm was off and my steps were clumsy. "Ni Mambo, did someone wake up on the wrong side of the bed?" she asked through her wireless microphone — to the whole room, but looking squarely at me.

Uuuuggggggh. I KNOW some of you feel me.

I stopped, picked up my step and returned it to the stack, and went down to the gym to shoot baskets — something my body understood. With basketball, I felt direction, confidence, and athletic. There was no discomfort in basketball for me. Nor was there discomfort in softball, waterskiing, rock climbing, or sex. For years I only took my body where it felt confident.

Volleyball? Nope. If I wasn't good at it, it wasn't happening. I could embody the ease and natural inclinations of some sports and movement, but rarely was I able to allow the discomfort of something new and unfamiliar in my body.

Now I see. I see where I would flee, and I see how as I got older and spent less time in active and athletic pursuits, my energy and attention accumulated in my head. Those thinking parts gave me a sense of control and certainty, until they didn't, and my body begged for my return, even if it was excruciatingly unfamiliar.

This is a digital image I created years ago. Many of my peers, friends, and even coaches have bought copies of this image. It's inspiring. It IS how my brain thinks — especially if you add an excessive amount of words to the colors and dots.

It's also a pretty dang good Freudian representation of how insignificant and ignored my body and her emotional burdens were at that time. It makes for a great piece of art, but not for a great embodied life.

In my mid-forties, just a few years after I drew this image, my hormones shifted and my work expanded, it was either succumb to a full body shut down, or find the courage to learn to be in my body. SLOW wasn't so much a choice at this time, my body *demanded* it of me. I got medical help, and I decided it was time to actually learn how to feel, to bring more of my energy into my body, instead of my colorful, reliable, and familiar head.

Learning to listen to and be in my body looks different from my dancy-dance, 5Rhythms, or official "Embodiment" friends, and it certainly isn't OM meditation, but I am more in my body than I have ever been. My breath and sensations are my guides. I'm finding my way, and what works for me.

I am learning.

I am unlearning.

I am sensating.

I am feeling my thoughts instead of just thinking them.

I am listening.

I am moving, shifting, stretching.

And on very rare occasions, even dancing.

My belly and hips hold wisdom.

My aches and pains guide me.

My body has a voice, she has stories, and she has direction.

My most basic biology has taught me more than any coaching or personal development.

My nervous system is foundational and it almost seems silly how many years I walked this earth without ever understanding her, seeing her, feeling her, listening to her.

My head is learning to become the tool of my body, and my body appreciates the full being expression of my mind, my heart, and especially the SELF energy I'm cultivating for her.

SELF-led
Body-held and felt
Heart fueled
Mind creatively expressed

# BE Energy

Everything is changing. Perfectly.

Becoming is here. Can you feel it? Or are you moving so fast you can't feel anything but the speed and striving?

Can you feel the welling up of your wandering heart? Or have you drowned it out with doing and rushing and nexting?

Your cells are calling for nourishment. Your nerves are yearning for grounding. Your heart wants to tuck self-judgment in her pocket of love with an extra cozy blanket, so it can rest and receive.

Listen. Listen instead of shouting.

What do you hear? What do you remember when you connect to your beating heart?

What is it that brings your flesh to life?

# BE Soul-FULL

There, can you feel it? When you slow down, way down, breathe, and sense? In between all the static and noise, beneath the heady thinking thoughts, down in the core of your body, is the voice. You know the one. And you know how it communicates — maybe with soft, whispered words, or with warm sensations in your body, or perhaps with vivid visions and images. It is always there — the part of you that *was* before you were born and will always *be*, even after your body has crumbled to dust.

Your infinite soul.

When I left the big company to start my own business, I heard that voice and felt that presence compelling me to decide. It took me four years to fully decide, and when I did, I named my LLC Soul-Full Living as an act of my intention. I had no idea what Soul-Full Living would actually require. I knew so very little of the apprenticeship to which I'd just bound myself.

When you decide to move to one neighborhood, and then decide you don't like it, you can change your mind. There may be some complications, but most decisions can be changed. When you DECIDE one of those Soul decisions — it will make space for the courage of yourSELF — it will call you forward into your becoming.

To give my resignation to my boss, I set a phone appointment with her at three o'clock on a Monday afternoon.

On Monday precisely at 3:00 p.m., I called, and her assistant told me she was not available.

We rescheduled for the following Monday.

I called the next Monday, again at 3:00 p.m., and her assistant, once more, told me she was not available.

We rescheduled for a third Monday.

That final Monday, at three o'clock, when her assistant told me she wasn't available, I told her to please pass on my resignation.

Within moments, my boss was on the phone, the boss who both esteemed me at times and who belittled and shamed me at others. The boss who taught me so much value, who knew how to manipulate and control the insecure parts of me who hungered for validation and affirmation, the boss who demanded loyalty. (I think it is totally manipulative when company culture demands loyalty. Integrity, yes. Demanding loyalty, though, is creepy and a sign of toxic work culture.)

That day, I'd quietly had a conversation with the little girl inside of me, the one that trembled at the thought of "not being good" and disappointing people, especially authority figures.

Long before I learned about the IFS framework, I gave calm and present SELF energy to the little seven-year-old in me. I told her, "Little girls don't have to make big business decisions, they don't need to have business or employment conversations, ever," and, I gave her permission to sit outside my office with my doggies while the wise, adult me made my call.

My stomach turned and I began to feel the moisture on the back of my neck and under my arms. I was telling the "Queen of Objection Handling" I was foregoing all the opportunities she gave me (hell-o, I earned it).

My boss began her skilled persuasive negotiations. She began to handle the objection that was me. And when she said, "I've done so much for you. Why on earth would you leave 105,000 agents, why would you leave the position and money we give you?"

From the presence and calm of my Soul SELF, I replied, "I'm not leaving you, I'm going toward me."

There was no objection in her book of scripts for that truth. She was silent, and then we completed the exit logistics and I hung up the phone. There is no manipulation or persuasion when a decision is made in the direction of one's Soul SELF.

The decision I made that day was more than a declaration of starting my own coaching practice and doing things my way instead of "following the model." I was both terrified and excited and knew I wouldn't-couldn't fail. I'd had enough of being dragged by others, and I stepped into the SELF of my own Soul and into the journey of discovering who I really was. Little did I know, the journey would be one of building SELF-trust and SELF-acceptance.

As I sit here after writing down this story that happened over a decade ago, viscerally feeling the memories in my whole being, remembering the certain and still insecure me who lived those moments, I lean back in my big-man desk chair, with my arms lifted behind my head, and I laugh a deep, satisfying laugh. There is a natural smile across my face. I can feel my eyes shining and tearing up. Here I am, living that dream of creating something true to my own Soul. Gawd, the business is juicy — my joy and delight. The BECOMING is my calling.

> "This is the first, wildest and wisest thing I know, that the soul exists, and that it is built entirely out of aliveness."
> - Mary Oliver

# BE Sovereign and SELF-Led

Something to ponder: Who does it benefit when you have to source validation from outside of you? Who does it benefit if you trust the systems instead of yourself? Who does it benefit if you are performing versus creating? Who does it benefit if you are taught to not feel, to comply, to not know all parts of yourself? And . . . What is the cost?

The invisible systems created us. Intentionally? Consciously? Willfully? Who knows — that one you get to decide for yourself. What I do know is that you and I have the opportunity to willfully, intentionally, and consciously discover and recreate ourselves.

I'm also not saying to throw out all of the systems and rules; the rules are not the ruler, they are the tools. *You* are the ruler, *you* get to decide, *you* can have sovereignty if you take it. Please realize, the invisible systems have conditioned you to NOT trust yourself to take it. It can be a wobbly journey. And you can survive the wobble. Liberation lives on the other side. Sovereignty lives on the other side.

I also know you to BE a benevolent RULER. I have no qualms about encouraging this SELF-CENTERED sovereignty, because you are not the kind of person who wakes up to screw people over and kill kittens or puppies. From your sovereignty, you don't owe anyone anything, *and* you will live and move in the world, within these existing systems, in a way that contributes and distributes more sovereignty to others. Leading your own life from SELF energy is the ultimate sovereignty. SELF-leadership is not about overcoming the difficulties we face, but instead, welcoming and leading all parts of us from that central core energy of SELF. SELF-Leadership builds SELF trust. Trusting yourself helps others trust themselves. SELF-leadership and SELF-trust aren't just about what we can get, they are also about who we end up being and what we end up giving to the world around us.

And who might benefit from that?

# BE Self Validation

In the soft light of my studio and office, here at my desk, settling in on a random Tuesday, I was in my usual ritual of being with my books, and journals, and pens, and yes, with a little social media here and there, sipping my vanilla coffee out of a favorite steel mug.

I'm was in a bit of a "wrestly" mode. Parts of me were in the heaviness of world events (mass shootings of children), parts of me were feeling agitated with the coachy world, and parts of me were demanding joy. Isn't that funny? Demanding joy, as if joy could be commanded any more than suffering.

Then two beautiful connections via social media happened for me. First, feeling a little melancholy as I was sipping my morning coffee, watching my sick dog eat grass — she was having a hard day — I was about to bypass some shit and MAKE myself feel joy when on Instagram, a post from Chris Zydel came across my feed. A gorgeous blooming pink and peach rose, with prose about how life here on Earth doesn't turn out how we want it to, and how the suffering of life shows up out of the blue. A gentle reminder from the first mentor who gave me permission to welcome all parts. She taught me and showed me that there is no time limit to the hard, and that sometimes, usually, it lasts longer than we want it to. The acknowledgement of the humanness of existing reminded me, deeply, to be SOFT with the HARD. The hard will release when it does. The joy will rise up when it does, and it is all part of this glorious thing we call living.

I breathed into being with what is: full compassion and calm. I took that softness to my journals and began to write, and then, as my ADHD brain does, I remembered a communication waiting for me in my messenger box (second connection).

Last year I was delighted to be asked to be a guest teacher in a former client's community. We've been planning this for months, and my session is in a few weeks. Her marketing materials were in my messenger box waiting for my sign-off. There was the header photo of my cute face with her fun psychedelic treatment, and then, there was her page. Instead of a sales page, she called it a recognition page.

In task mode I began to read, thinking I would knock this one thing off my to-do list for the day. And there, on what is traditionally a page full of what I call big-box-coaching sales copy, were stories of me and how this woman experienced me. She called it a recognition page:

> *". . . an equality and neutrality . . ."*

> *". . . allowing for me and my baby and the interruptions . . ."*

> *". . . slicing through bullshit by just being herself . . ."*

> *"Her beingness extends permission to everyone else to be who they are too . . . "*

> *"Allison's field is both spacious and cozy; she tends a fire inside of her that extends her generosity of spirit to anyone who even follows her on social media."*

> *". . . sovereign support . . . this queen lives it, gets it, and gives it."*

Not one ounce of big-box-coaching copy. No performative or overused descriptors. I felt so specifically seen.

*This space is intentional . . . let's take a breath in this space . . . and meet and receive that deep desire to be so genuinely seen.*

The connection I felt in reading her words unhooked me from the mainline feed of malarkey that I so often step into. Gawd, don't we all just want to be seen and appreciated so deeply? I can't speak for you, but I'm slowly, stitch by stitch, undoing the bamboozlement of "BE BIG, PLAY BIG" bullshit the self-improvement world puts on us.

Parts of me buy into this story. Parts of me believe that I continually Scorpio-sting myself with self-sabotage (yes, my astrology and limiting beliefs say this), by being less than my potential perfection . . . as if who I am right now isn't lovely and enough.

When I look with the eyes and heart of my true SELF, though, the only sting I see is that we don't delight in our being exactly as we are in this moment. That we need another to remind us of our brilliance, instead of remembering on our own. It's only ever the thought that we're doing it wrong that hurts.

Be soft with the hard, and remember, you are a delight, especially when you are being just you.

# BE Boundaries

Exiles are not only wounded inner-child parts of us. Once upon a time, they were eager and held an immense vitality and innocence. They were unboundaried children before the wounds, before the trauma. They were young, honest energy beings.

Again my mind sees the child in the *Still Face Experiment*. When her mother withdrew her energetic presence and connection, yet still being physically present, the baby had three specific instinctive responses: 1) She leaned toward her mother, fawned, and tried to be pleasing enough to restore the connection. 2) When that didn't work, she got angry, fussy, and almost rebellious. 3) When the mother still didn't connect, the baby dissolved and turned inside.

These yearnings for restoring connection turn into the coping mechanisms of over-functioning, rebelling, and under-functioning.

The irony of my lifetime of armored living is that my armors presented themselves as open-hearted, as giving, as contributing.

Hello, Fawning and People-Pleasing parts. I see your motive was to maintain connection — such presentable armor. You were stealthy and able to hide behind the praise and acknowledgement you generated. Your coping behavior of over-functioning seemed like it would protect us by fixing everything around us so that people would stay.

Hello, Regret part. I see you holding hands with Shame and Blame. Together you are all concerned that the past vacuum of thirst is actually what drove countless loved-ones away. I see your sadness and I hear your warnings for the future. Your concerns make sense. I can also see how each of you then, and now, are just trying to keep me from being unloved, being unchosen, and being left by loved ones. I see all the connections you are showing me. I see the connections to your pain, and your fears, and how you adapted with people-pleasing and over-functioning in order to be safe.

When these parts took on their roles, they were young. I was young. They didn't have the wisdom that comes with age (or studying attachment theory).

When I really listen to these parts, instead of shoving or shaming them away, I can see how in the past, with these parts *leading* my life, I gave myself *no chance* to be me, because so much energy was put into managing the opinions and emotions of others — an ultimately impossible task.

I can feel the thirst in my chest, the dehydration in my cells from a lifetime of bleeding into the responsibilities of others, as a means of attempting my desperate longing for true connection.

Again, no fault, just reasons. And, these parts did a pretty good job with what they had. It worked until it didn't.

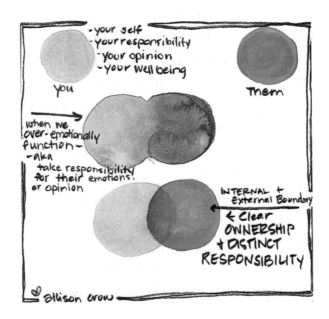

From this place of fully seeing (when I am in even a small amount of SELF energy), I can update these parts, and together we can alleviate their concerns in a few ways: We build trust through connection, compassion, and my listening to them; from SELF, I will update them to my current age and capabilities; and when they are ready, we will figure out, together, their updated roles. Once they are updated, we will get clear about our distinct responsibilities, and what is not ours to fix, so that we can decide, together, on the internal and external boundaries we will create.

SELF-led instead of parts-led. Unarmored, but boundaried.

Many of the people I work with, because our energies align, seem to also have spent so much of their lives in the center of this image, for the same fundamental reasons I did. And together we are learning boundaries. We are learning to notice what is ours, and what is not. We are slowing down and connecting with the oldest cravings and unmet needs in us, and we are listening.

I am now fifty, and boundaries feel so new to me. I certainly am no expert and have only recently allowed myself to receive support around understanding how to "BE boundaried." I have yet to amass a collection of books, or even follow the boundary experts, on social media. I have spent a season with a dear friend and fellow recovering people pleaser who has become an expert at boundaries. Shanti Zimmerman, in her human and relational way, is one of my mentors and a fellow way-finding soul. When I spent six weeks in her coaching container, what struck me deeply was the SELF-validation piece. This permission to advocate for ourselves, our parts, our exiles within boundaries is what creates safety. A totally open heart is like an innocent child. In the wisdom of our age and experience, we can be open and yet still hold ownership and boundaries that create safety and allow us to connect wholeheartedly with others.

Trauma had me armor up my heart, healing is teaching me to open it up, with better and better boundaries every day. Living to the wild edges means giving up "either/or" and absolutes. It means building the skills of navigating nuance. It means consciously using protective means at the right time and in the right place, and then setting them down again when it is safe.

COURAGE

# RememBEr

When I am armored up, when I am in protective mode, hustling mode, parts-led mode, and chasing mode, I am forgetting. My own psyche make-up of (nature+nurture+trauma+choices+systemic privileges) leaves me predisposed to forgetting. The world we live in is set up to cause us to forget our true nature and power. Marketing, media, news, toxic capitalism, politics, schools, religion — everywhere I look I can't unsee how we are conditioned to forget, lulled by the onslaught of teaching, advertisements, and information that causes us to forget our authority and autonomy.

When we forget, we give away our power. We give away our inner desires and bend in ways that keep us quiet, complacent, and submissive. When we forget, we buy shit we don't need for the dopamine hit. When we forget, we slip into comparison and competition, and it sucks the life out of our creative souls. We armor up in protective gear and live in coping and numbing behaviors. We suffer.

RememBEring is the state of remembering who we BE at our core and essence, and embodying that in life and creation. It is not eliminating the difficult, the fears, or the discomforts. It is a shift, though — from BEING that suffering, to RememBEring we are SOUL. RememBEring we are SELF-energy, ready and able to BE with and lead all parts. In RemeBEring, we can be in our bodies and in our humanness.

I believe the spirit of my authentic Self existed and exists in the Great Infinite Everywhere across all time and space. She came to be embodied in the human experience that is my life. She is the fullness of my being. She is clarity, creativity, love, presence, courage, peace, playfulness, and self-trust. She is compassionate and validating with grief, anger, sadness, and all the emotions at the edge of life. She moves in a state of flow and because she is centered and full, everything in her orbit is touched and impacted by her being.

RememBEring is that I am BEING in the state of her and she is me.

My belief is that she has always been in my essence; she is timeless, and in that aspect — the living of life buried in unconscious bias, human conditioning, and mass-fucking-media, and information overstimulation — I sometimes forget her.

Through my experience of living out of alignment and the inauthenticity of being an excessive people pleaser, I discovered deep soul-disturbing discomfort. I was not really being me. This discomfort sent me to the path of self-discovery. I began to question what I had been told was really true. I began to listen within, to search, and to experiment. Through listening, searching, and experimenting, I started to both remember and discover who I really came here to BE.

When I remember my essence, I am emboldened to be sourced by her, to behave and move in alignment with her, and discover things shift for the better in my life, especially internally. It is here I am aligning my authentic SELF with how I walk and talk and BE in the world. It's both a simple and a complex journey, simple because everything I am is already within me, and complex because it seems to be scattered in both wounded and protective parts of me, and those parts are relentless with their desire to protect me.

Our creative-life-filled-soul is the ultimate joy and freedom, but some parts experience this as dangerous to the internal system. Once you have realized the joy and innate aliveness of RememBEring, you can't *not* want to spread it to the people you love and care about. I love my individual RememBEering, but it is imperative that I acknowledge for all of us that RememBEering is only possible from a nervous system state of safety.

You and I have the luxury of having our basic needs met. We have the time, space, and money to read personal development and inspirational books, and yes, my book is for you. For us, and in service of the greater-connected-US, I have to acknowledge that so many people both systemically (poor and marginalized in any way) and individually (lived experience), don't have the luxury of having their basic needs met. RememBEering is absolutely a luxury available to those of us living with our basic safety and psychological needs met. So many humans aren't afforded the ability to live day-to-day in nervous system safety. Maslow's Hierarchy of Needs is the clearest visual description I can offer to help us see:

I've taken the liberty of adding a few extra fulfillment needs and psychological needs from my creative and metaphysical studies over the years, thus, the title "Maslow's Hierarchy of Needs +Plus."

I've spoken before about how *in my head* I've been for so long. I notice a compassionate smile cross my face when I see that I was striving so hard to create psychological needs and fulfillment needs, when I had some gaping holes in my basic needs. I was striving to live open-hearted but without many of my safety needs being met, especially nervous system regulation. This left me often feeling like shit, and at times, treating other people, and my communities like shit. RememBEr isn't just in the mind, it is also in the body and nervous system. It isn't just in me, it is in the US.

In the RememBEring, we restore and heal not only for our own independent morality, life, and/or expansion, but also for the contribution to the horizontal impact on the greater US. My personal work helps me BE the person that contributes to the communities and societies around me: social, civic, and human race. My personal values and morals are more horizontal than vertical these days. The school and religion of my youth taught me vertical morality to the exclusion of everything else, and it left me forgetting my true and whole nature.

RememBEring is the home in my own heart that is connected, not only to the divine, but to everything and everyone on the horizons of this earth. I may forget time and time again, and it is my intention to RememBEr.

# BE Creativity

Somewhere in my mid to late forties, I crossed a line I didn't know I was approaching. I didn't even realize crossing that line was exactly what I had been making so much effort toward for all these years.

The line I crossed was from protection to creation. I moved from defense to offense. My Gawd, I was even taught as a high school basketball player that defense won the game. My dad, from the moment we were in the back seat of the car with him, was singing the praises of defensive driving. These were both legitimate for their intended purposes, but don't translate so well to living a glorious and human life. Looking back, I can see so fucking clearly how most of the movement in my being and in the world came from defensive, reactive, and protective intentions.

Before the line, I was mostly led by my protectors — the parts of me that set out to make sure I was safe and loved in the world. They watched the world around me, all 360 degrees, and anticipated rejection, being left, being criticized, and being unloved. They kept me awake at night, overthinking in anxiety about things I could not control. They shut me down with depression when my nervous system didn't know how to take in the overstimulation of everyday life.

I knew these parts were there, I just didn't see their roles. I saw them as my diseases and faults, my weaknesses even. Chase, chase, perform, strive, thirst . . . a perpetual state of dehydration in energy. When I began to shift, literally, through art, somatic work, and most recently IFS parts work, I experienced the power of creation instead of the struggle of performance. I'm thankful to my client, Cari, and her parts, for this distinction.

We can perform ad nauseam — and it is never enough.

Or we can create — and the energies to create are infinite, they are source-driven, honor process, and allow for rest.

Can you notice the difference in energies? Performance with perfection at all costs is gripping, it is draining, and it is depleting. It's the avoiding, yet also the carrying of shame and pain. Creativity is boundless, expansive, and energizing. It is sourced from the infinite being within you. Nurture that source. Play. Rest. Create. Enjoy. You are more than enough and always have been.

# BE the Decider

I learned the concept of "abundance thinking" when I first was introduced to mindset coaching in the real estate industry. This fantastical idea of being able to create abundance through my thinking was fascinating and alluring. I spent the next chunk of my life studying, teaching, reading, and listening to all things abundance. And guess what? None of it ever solved my money woes — the ones in my head or in my bank accounts.

For a lifetime — inherited from my family, and continued on in my own way of being as an adult — I was stressed and mostly miserable around money. Money was constantly on the brain and if you were to take a look in there, this is the pinball game you would have seen and heard:

Will I ever get out of debt?

Will I ever have the money for my taxes?

Am I charging enough and is all this business stuff really worth it if it includes all this financial strife?

How have I made so much money, and yet have so little left?

Why is it so easy for others and so fucked up for me?

I held shame about money I'd carelessly spent and could never get back. I had an accountant, money coaches, and a bookkeeper, and I knew my numbers. No matter what I made, though, and even if I paid down debt, there was always the dang April tax bill. One of my coaches called it a quality problem and still, that perspective shift didn't help. I gave, gave, and over-gave, thinking that some law of money would bring it right back to me like a boomerang, because that is what I'd been told in church and in the woo-woo world.

It was miserable. No matter how wonderful life was, the money misery was always there.

One day I was at a retreat as a client. One of my own clients was there, too. As I recall, we'd all just finished a session about money and worth. A curious thought crossed my mind. I'd known Stacy P for a few years. I knew her to be wealthy and able to create money at will for the things she desired for herself and her family. She worked joyfully and delighted in providing private education to her kids, a lovely home for her family in California, and even a Tesla for herself. I also knew her to have glorious designer clothes and shoes. Not once had she come with a money issue to coaching, nor did she ever use terms rampant in the coaching industry around either "scarcity" or "abundance." There was no smell of either boasting nor efforting in her essence around money.

So I asked her: "Stacy, I know you to be wealthy, and I'd like to ask you a question — that is probably pretty personal and private if I may?"

"Of course." She smiled and opened her genuine heart.

"Well, I have a new hypothesis regarding 'money mindset' I'd like to run by you. I imagine that you, because you BE wealthy, don't actually THINK about abundance or money mindset. Also, that your beliefs and identity around money don't ever effort or stir anxiety in you, and that THAT is the actual money mindset to have. One so sure, that it isn't even a thought. Wealthy people don't try to have an abundant mindset, do they?"

From the coziness of the sofa, she smiled big and gracefully pulled her feet up onto the edge of the coffee table to display her gorgeous shoes and said, "That is EXACTLY right, and I'm so wealthy GUCCI sends ME Christmas gifts," she said with a wink.

It was playful, not an ounce of ego, and just her ISness. No efforting.

That day I decided to stop thinking about "trying to create abundance" and start acting and BEING my version of wealthy. I decided that wealthy people allocate their money wisely. They save and invest and live within their means, even with indulgences. I opened up what I call my "Shitty Profit First" accounts (aka I do it in a way that works for me — all in one bank versus in separate banks) and every Friday I started allocating my money in a plan that worked for me. I decided. I became THE DECIDER. I decided to BE wealthy and wise with money through actions and behavior. Instead of thinking abundance, I just decided to do the math and act accordingly. I decided to make different money decisions instead of winging it with "abundance thinking."

Within a year the debt was gone, and a tax account was funded with each payment of income — never again have I had to put my taxes on a credit card. The cash is there, because I put it there. I decided to sell my expensive house and moved to one that was way below my means, still living gloriously. My retirement is building, and my investments are compounding. My income is still in the same general range, and money just is. Money and I do math and allocations weekly. We set and follow plans. We just are wealthy. We don't think about it. We don't worry about it. We DO it because we decided.

I've been coaching professionally for a looooong time. I started in my early thirties and somehow I ended up in my fifties, and I'm still here. Countless times people have requested of me, "I need someone to kick my ass," or, "I need accountability."

We have been so conditioned to have someone else decide for us. To have the pressure put on us from the outside, laden with shame, rejection, or punishment.

Think about that for a moment or two. Feel it in your being.

No. I won't kick your ass, or hold you accountable. You decide. You choose. YOU DECIDE. YOU CHOOSE.

You are The Decider.

You are the one who lays your head on your pillow. You are the one who lives in your body. You are the one who has your family, and friends, and life. You Choose. You are The Decider. Do not give that sovereignty away. And if like me, you have lived a life of other-sovereign, now is your time to take it back. Take. It. Back.

Yes, it is the ultimate responsibility to decide. It is the ultimate power to be The Decider. The world taught you to give all that responsibility and power to others with sneaky moves. That set you up — that set me up — for abandoning ourselves over and over, and when you BE the Decider, you never have to leave yourself again. Because of the muscle memory of your bones and being, the decision is just the start. You will have to decide over and over, and you will have to practice, and build the skills and new practices that will help you embody that decision.

I'm here to help you learn to trust yourself, and to cultivate the capacity and skills to self-create the life and work you desire. Your soul-full life does not have to be created with beating or shame or criticism or threats. Even when there is a time to be direct and clear, that can be done with compassion instead of a jagged blade. I won't do it to you. You don't do it to you.

Yes, we need one another as humans. Still yourself, primarily source from your core SELF, strengthen within yourself, validate yourself, build trust, and then use that trust with yourself as the foundation for collaboration and co-creation with the people around you.

Be the Decider.

# BE Settled

In my dreams, I'm not ever in a fancy hotel or a swanky luxury location. I'm certainly not in a formal dress and heels. Never in my real dreams did I dream of wealth the way it is sold to me. Never in my dreams am I a manager of a large staff and team. Never in my dreams did I want to build something and sell it for millions.

Never.

In my dreams, I'm in old boot-cut jeans and cowboy boots, and a soft, natural-fiber, white T-shirt. My hair is wild, or perhaps in a hat. My smile is wide and there is light in my green eyes. I might have a flannel tied at my waist if the Texas air is cool. The ground beneath my feet is dirt or grass . . . a rescue dog or three at my side. Willie Nelson is on the radio and my paid-for, eight-year-old F-150 is my ride.

In my dreams, I'm in the Texas hill country with scrappy cedars, Texas wildflowers, and big blue skies . . . the stars at night are big and bright . . . *clap, clap, clap*. Well, you know how the song goes. And my pool. There's my pool. And my man, and laughter at the dumbest things.

In my dreams more is not better, and luxury cars and homes, high fees, and global impact never show up. In my dreams, I never am rescuing the world. I'm simply living in it, paying attention to the details because I'm going slow, writing prose, and poems, and watching birds in my backyard.

In my dreams, more is not better. And interestingly, just like my business tagline, in my dreams, BETTER is better.

In my dreams, perhaps I see an inspiring and sorta-best-selling (at least amongst my peoples) book or two, more than enough business doing what I love with people I know deeply and well. Sharing my heart, showing my work. Sharing, out loud, shit that most people don't dare to say. Sharing softness and sovereignty from the inside out.

Slinging paint, reading books, and journaling the gazillion thoughts in my head. Drinking way too much Diet Coke and Bota Box RedVolution wine, and consuming way too few green vegetables. Holding my own heart and belly in profound care and SELF-leadership, and guiding others in the same skills of internal care, emotional leadership, and generative creativity.

Slow-growth-cultivation is rare and deep.

In my real dreams, there aren't too many people. There aren't thousands, or even hundreds. My dreams hold a handful of people at any given time. There is no scale or seven-figure-year-after-year plan. My clients aren't the most notorious, successful, or most famous but they are grounded, holy-human, with an urge to create and cultivate and connect deeply instead of performing.

Eleven years and one week ago I left the go-big-or-go-home dreams the company had for me, and I set out on my own. I'll be damned if part of me continually gets hooked into the play so many others are making. Seven figures, and CEO, and change-maker, impact, and whatever else.

I've woven everything in and out, trying on different versions of me carrying the world's definition of my success, holding myself in painful comparison to my peers because somewhere along the way that dream that others had bled into my bones with the allure of belonging. In so many moments, parts of me have believed the more-more-more capitalistic lies. That play is glamorous and seductive and in no way wrong for those who want it.

But have you ever tried to plant hydrangeas in the rocky and sandy soil of central Texas? They can't thrive. I'm a wildflower. For forty-nine years I tried to outgrow my native soul by doing anything and everything except completely surrendering to the native soil I am here to grow in.

I am a wildflower who is meant to grow and thrive in a climate of her very own. I make plenty of money. In fact I wrote more business in a single month this year than I ever have in any other month. That money will come and go and months from now it won't matter. Money always comes and goes.

Recently, I also helped my mom and dad sell their home of fifty-two years. The home of my birth and youth, and a million memories for our family. With both skill and care, I helped my parents navigate the toughest emotional decisions and pick a new place to live, a place where neither of them ever dreamed of living. I *mostly* held my own heart and theirs with grace, and calm, hopeful, but unattached. What I'm more proud of than the cash, is the care and connection I was able to give my parents. And we aren't done yet. Let the packing up of all those years begin!

When I told one of my coaches I was spending the rest of the year loving on my family and the clients I have, he rolled his eyes at me and said I was "settling." At first, I was pissed. I certainly didn't feel seen . . . but he's right.

I am SETTLED. It is SETTLED. Not in the limiting belief way, but in the deeply settled in the sovereignty of my own soul and knowing. I AM SETTLED.

I am here, leaving the "freeway and fast lane" for the last time. I'm settled in my soul and taking the scenic route of a hill country road, planted in this native soil, the soil of being casual, deep coaching conversations, art, writing, dogs, family, and swimming . . . right here in this small plot of central Texas land with my paid-for old truck, my right-sized roster of clients, and my man. I'm the wealthiest woman I know.

PS: I terminated the contract with the coach who accused me of settling.

# BE Practicer

The work of becoming unarmored, of holding all that life brings us, and creating all we desire to create, is not a one-time event. It's not even a series of events. It's not just about creating the life or work you want (although that was the trailhead, for me, of this work). It truly is a journey, and, one without a destination, really. My Gawd, the mind wants a destination. It's not just about peeling back the layers of the onion — such an elementary metaphor for the intricate and nuanced experience of living.

This work is practice — messy, ongoing, intentional practice. We don't embrace and practice because we want to achieve more — or even because we want to become something that we aren't, like an escape. Practice isn't about striving — it's about our natural becoming. We need to embrace practice because life requires it. Any achievement accomplished, or performance completed, is just a moment — a blip of time that will pass in the next moment. The dopamine wears off and a new day shows up with different weather and another blank page.

The flickering blue-lights, red notifications, hypnotizing prizes of your devices will glorify the dopamine hits to sell you stuff. But your Soul knows that being the ever-curious student and the willing practicer will sustain you all the way to the edges of this wild and glorious life.

Choose your practices with intention. Know what enlivens you, what restores you, what depletes you, and what entices you to forget who you truly BE. Know what invites you to rememBEr. And practice. Seemingly mundane practice will create your miracles.

Practice the things that cause you to rememBEr.

# BE Community

We don't live in a silo — this work is for us, yes, but we are commingled with others, with our communities, with animals, plants, seas, forests, and skies. We are inextricably connected with this earth, with the infinite spirit realm, and with humanity. Our individual willingness to embrace and practice being fully alive, exploring all of our humanness, is the ultimate act of the faith I almost decided to not believe in.

Parts of me repeat the learned mantras of, "Don't be so self-absorbed."

This work of becoming unarmored requires me to turn inward, over and over. I am keenly aware, and incessantly feel, that the more I listen to and care for the protectors and exiles in my own system, the more I can see the protectors and exiles in the communities and humans around me. Something in me is becoming softer in the best ways, and my strength is spreading from my head and muscles deep into my bones, and then grounding into the earth. Grounded. Soft. Able. The care I have is becoming less frantic, less thirsty, more solid.

The sturdiness allows me to drop beneath the noise and take collected steps in my caring for the communities and world around me. Ideas become embodied action — even if it is the tiniest action. From this place, I trust even the small steps taken in the direction of better. Perhaps these small steps aren't as exciting as frothing anger in the name of justice out into the abyss of Twitter. That may create a temporary dopamine hit, but it isn't sustainable, it's fucking exasperating.

Each step of care I take for myself and my parts, gives me the courage and stamina to take a step or two out in the world around me.

> "The more we begin to matter to ourselves, the more the wellbeing of others can matter to us."
>
> — Matt Kahn [24]

# BE Self-Trust

My unhinged summer nearly took me down this year. Day after day, crying, waking up anxious in the middle of the night, and then eventually finding my calm only to get tripped up by the slightest provocation would send me into flooded emotions and a dysregulated nervous system. Parts-led again by the most tender, angry, disappointed, and afraid parts of me, I found myself considering a full-on quit.

I remember the moment I first deeply opened up the door of self-trust. It was in the Denton days, probably around 2015 and the usual business and life stressors were piling up around me. After worrying for a few days, I took myself out to the back yard, and I laid on the grass. My body was being held by the earth, my gaze up through the leaves of the two hundred year old oak, to the sky.

It occurred to me from the deepest place of knowing that I'd had a lifetime of worry, and the problems of life would continually come, but that I had always figured things out, ALWAYS! Time on task has proved it to me, over and over. In that moment, instead of solving the problems at hand, I let my body and mind fill with the truth: I knew that I could trust myself.

I can trust myself.

That day, I felt the fullness of this, and my perspective shifted, not only with the worldly problems of tax bills and leaking windows, but this knowledge gave me the courage to go deeper into the full-body and emotional work that was waiting for me.

Because I practice SELF-trust, and I now know trust takes time on task, when the thoughts of wanting to quit show up — it is my reminder to absofuckinglutely do my nourishing practices, starting with taking a walk.

**Self-Trust in real time:**

On a walk one recent morning, the power struggle of two loud parts, a firefighter and a manager, ran through my head. It went like this:

> Cynical and Discouraged Frothing firefighter: "Why in the hell do I keep pulling this thread of personal development and navel gazing?"

> Coachy Self-talk Contrived Hope manager: "Because you can't not, and you know it always ends up good."

> Cynical and Discouraged Frothing firefighter: "Oh for Fuck's sake. Plenty of people don't do all this inquiry and are fine. I'm quitting and just going to do the Jimmy Buffett thing and drink margaritas and sing songs on beaches and have no worries. I might even take up smoking cigarettes — really long skinny ones."

> Coachy Self-talk Contrived Hope manager: "First off, your skin would get leathery and you'd get all wrinkly like a dried prune, and your liver and lungs would corrode, so NO."

> Cynical and Discouraged Frothing firefighter: "This is insane. The thread just keeps unraveling. Unraveling life, unraveling all your beliefs, and you just keep finding stuff that causes suffering. Can't we just cauterize the thread with a flame and walk away. We can quit the

business, and just sell art or something. Or maybe get a job again."

Coachy Self-talk Contrived Hope manager: "You know you don't do well with the restraints of a job — those ideas are really extreme. Get your shit together."

Thankfully the presence of nature, the lack of a pixelated device, and the exertion of my walk helped me exasperate these two polarized parts. That weariness and my willingness to hear them out made way for space to take a breath of Presence and SELF-energy.

Feeling the sense of SELF-energy from my core, I noticed the warmth of my heart and a whisper of my Soul: *"I am here with you. Of course this journey is tremendously difficult at times. I will not leave you. It's OK to rest, and, you remember, this is the work we came to do — we came to have an animated and full life, these threads make up the fabric — it's so truly beautiful, exquisite really. You can trust yourself to experience it all. We are, each moment, in the art and craft of Soul-Full Living. Soul, Spirit, Self, Mind, Body . . . all these wide experiences of life. Darling, never let go of the thread."*

# BE Spirit

Somewhere in the writing of this book, I acknowledged the season of my spiritual journey exploring my complete humanness. Humanness was, for the last few years of my life, my religion, my ritual, my laboratory. Not that I planned it this way, but how could I be a stand for transparent leadership without fully allowing all my humanness? Perhaps it was because for so many years my spiritually was one of my primary protective ways of avoiding discomfort, my biggest bypass and dissociation.

Walking this path of not escaping my flesh has been glorious and intense. I didn't intentionally reject the Spirit realm, but something, probably *from* the Spirit realm, called me to my biology, my psychology, to nature, science, to the math of me and the world around me. It seduced me out of the spiritual chakras of my third eye and crown, and down to my roots — to discover and be with the ecology of me. I chuckle now, because my early spiritual-not-religious-awakening started in my second, sacral, chakra, and for years, the root chakra — family, origin, history, safety, and security — didn't resonate with me. I was allured by the magic of the spiritual realms. And yet, life called me back exactly there, to my roots, my home, and not just the literal home on Bowman Avenue in Austin, Texas, but the entire home of me and all of the parts of my internal family.

One of my early favorite authors, Thomas Moore, in *The Re-Enchantment of Everyday Life*[25] wrote, "We may have to return to childhood and recover its truths, its vision, its logic, its sense of time and space, its extraordinary cosmology, and its creative physics if we want a way out of the black-and-white world of disenchantment."

Was it the writing of this book? Was it the deeeeeeep IFS work and meeting of some of my most hidden, shamed, and volatile parts? Was it learning presence with them instead of fixing? Was it the last five months of navigating my dad's stroke, my parents downsizing from our family home of fifty-two years, and being in the thick of family history, present, and future? Was it the leaning into professional and financial self-trust that I had to do in order to take the space to care for my parents and myself this season? Was it the illuminating and albeit overwhelming ADHD diagnosis, or the hormones of perimenopause? Was it the anxiety attack that sent me to the hospital thinking I was having a heart attack? Was it the goddamned ninety days of one hundred plus degree heat and humidity in Texas that started two months earlier this year than it ever has before? Was it the allowing of grief avoided for fifty years to literally break my heart with an NSTEMI heart attack as I finish this last chapter of this very book? Who knew that the unhinged pain of this last summer would be my secret ally.

I am almost certain the journey of meeting and being with my own inner ecology is not complete, but there was a special shift that happened this very week. Its timing is not lost on me as I'm literally in the last few days of writing before I pass this manuscript off to my publisher.

My husband and I were watching our "shows," as we often do in the evenings. There was a scene in *Five Days at Memorial*[26] where a husband prays for his wife. I don't know the exact script, but I'll share the way I remember it, the way it touched me to the core, root chakra and all:

> "God wrap your arms around us, keep us safe, and may we follow your light."

Gently, softly — just like I needed, that prayer physically went through me and my heart sensed it was once again fully reconnected with Spirit. Not in the traditional ways of shame or repentance like the prodigal daughter, but more like the releasing of something, that was for a time, withheld for our own good.

Spirit whispered to me, "Now. Now you know how to never leave yourself again. Well done, little one, wise one, all parts of you, well done."

# *Epilogue*

I do not find it coincidental that as I came to the end of creating this book, I both had the reconnection with Spirit I was seeking, and then, fifteen days later, a NSTEMI heart attack.

After a 6:00 a.m. ambulance ride, I spent two nights and three full days in the hospital. Test after test, EKGs, bloodwork (so much bloodwork), I still have residue from the electrodes placed all over my body for both constant monitoring and the stress test. My EKGs were clear; my stress tests and images showed no clogged arteries. My echocardiogram was perfect. My bloodwork, twenty-four hours after the event, did show alarming measurements of troponin. Troponin is a protein that shows up in the blood when there has been damage to your heart. The doctors, mystified regarding the cause, eventually sent me home with a diagnosis of Non-ST-Elevation Myocardial Infarction (NSTEMI).

Here is how the Cleveland Clinic defines this heart event: "A NSTEMI is a type of heart attack that usually happens when your heart's need for oxygen can't be met. This condition gets its name because it doesn't have an easily identifiable electrical pattern like the other main types of heart attacks."[27]

Discharge instructions involved a few meds, the typical heart-healthy diet and exercise practices, a follow-up with the cardiologist in two weeks, and a "return to normal activity" directive.

I am not a doctor, this is not medical advice, and I certainly could be wrong, but I KNOW what happened to me. The body always knows. Of course I am taking all the medical advice of the professionals, and when I listen to me, I hear the intuitive wisdom of my lived experience over the last season. I can see the emotional pain I've processed in the last few months, some of it circumstantial, and much of it, the lifetime of grief and loss I've avoided feeling.

I don't feel a "wake-up" call. I feel an acknowledgement from my body, that my heart did in fact suffer temporary damage, because, especially, these last few months, I courageously felt to the edges of my now, and to the depths of my trauma history. My heart muscle was and is strained by the extra emotional stress. Sometimes we experience trauma as something that happens to us, and sometimes we experience trauma as something that *doesn't* happen to us. During this recent season of processing old burdens and past trauma, I have been fully resourced both personally and professionally. I gently let my heart hold it all from this fully resourced place. I walked the talk of what this book is about. I've met, and connected with, so many parts of me, that for years, were pressed down and shoved away. I've welcomed all parts of me. My heart let me know she sees my work, and she has given me the gift of an obvious reminder to nurture her deeply.

I feel I've lived my own personal experience of Kintsugi. Kintsugi is the centuries-old art of repairing broken pottery with gold. These broken vessels are not only still seen as useful, but also beautiful — not in spite of the cracks, but because of the cracks. They also say the repairs make the pottery ultimately stronger. My life — all our lives — is the pottery, the cracks, and the gold, all at once.

Post discharge, the doctors don't tell you about the natural anxiety and grief the experience of even a mild heart attack can bring. I was calm and centered in the hospital, and the last few days at home have been a range of physical, emotional, and mental states. This is what needs recovery — not just my heart muscle. When they say, "avoid stress," they don't compassionately let you know that making follow-up visits and coordinating care across all of your providers will be an absolute pain in the ass.

So yes, my anxiety has been present, my sensitivities are activated, my system perceives a threat. My once three-prescription life has — for a while — turned to a seven-prescription life. Trying to remember when to take them all is an adjustment. Transitions are wobbly. I know how to wobble, though.

This morning, yes, this very morning as I complete this manu-script, I had one last image to share with you because of a healing experience I had with a friend, whose partner also recently had a heart attack.

My friend reached out with a loving video, and despite my tension and overwhelm, I decided to call him on FaceTime. I am reminded that healing of any kind truly does require connection. Connection heals more than any information. As his calming presence (not his words) came through the video, there with me, I literally FELT the truth that attunement with myself and others is what heals. I felt my nervous system shift. No armor. No protection. No manager. No Xanax. Not even breathwork or meditation (and those are super helpful) would have brought me to a clear, calm, and joy-full center this morning like presence and attunement did.

Connection
Is
Everything.

EPILOGUE

That second grade little girl who wanted to offer the prayer of relationship in school chapel knew . . . she KNEW, and she created this work, and this last image is for herself, and for you.

# Endnotes & References

## Part I: Cultivation

1  Goldsmith, Marshal., Clester, Shane. *What Got You Here Won't Get You There: The graphic edition*. Writers of the Round Table Press; Illustrated edition (August 20, 2013).
2  The name of the student referenced in the story "Art Is Life" in Part I: Cultivation has been changed to protect their anonymity.
3  Clear, James. *Atomic Habits*. New York, Penguin Random House LLC, 2018
4  Schwartz, Richard C, *Introduction to The Internal Family Systems Model*, Trailheads Publications, (2001).

## Part II: Connection

5  Gabor Maté "CI Workshop with Gabor" (CI Workshop Part 2, Compassionate Inquiry Self-Study Online Course, Compassionate Inquiry Workshop Video, Vancouver, 2018).
6  Zero To Three, and UMass Boston, "Still Face Experiment." YouTube video, 8:33, 2007 and 2010, https://www.youtube.com/watch?v=vmE3NfB_HhE
7  "What is Internal Family Systems," *IFS Institute*. Updated 2022. https://ifs-institute.com/
8  "Richard C. Schwartz, Ph.D. The Founder of Internal Family Systems." *IFS Institute*. Updated 2022. https://ifs-institute.com/about-us/richard-c-schwartz-phd
9  To find out more in-depth about IFS and coaching, please visit my personal IFS resources page. https://allisoncrow.com/ifs/
10 Dodson, William. "How ADHD Ignites Rejection Sensitive Dysphoria." *ADDitude*, Updated August 30, 2022. https://www.additudemag.com/rejection-sensitive-dysphoria-and-adhd/
11 Heather Doyle Fraser, Publisher, Writer, Coach. https://www.cmcollab.com/heather-doyle-fraser
12 Townes, Deidra (August 28, 2022) *Becoming a leader is synonymous with becoming yourself. It is precisely that simple and also that difficult.* [Status update]. Facebook. https://www.facebook.com/dctowns/posts/pfbid029LGDhUcKQRMVtcg3Rdewe31BZSNT-9P96eLXsHC3KfxGWV4MnYuMAppwZkCTqYA9NI

## Part III: Calm

13   Behavioral Down is a canine calming and training technique originated by Mark McCabe of *Training Behind the Ears.* https://www.markmccabe.com/wp-content/uploads/2019/07/BD-2019-rev_compressed-1.pdf

14   Dodson, Dale. "Harry's Behavior — HGD Reactive vs. Cognitive" Email. 2022 https://www.happygentledogs.com/

15   https://www.havening.org/

16   *Chödrön*, Pema, *Pema Chödrön: What to Do When You Lose It Completely*, YouTube video, 2:13. February 10, 2016.

17   *A Thief In The Night*, directed by Donald W. Thomson (Mark IV Pictures, 1972), https://www.imdb.com/title/tt0070795/

18   Kahn, Matt, *Whatever Arises, Love That: A Love Revolution That Begins With You*. Sounds True, (2016).

19   Loehr, James E, and Schwartz, Tony. *The Power of Full Engagement: Managing Energy, Not Time Is the Key to High Performance and Personal Renewal*, Free Press (2005).

## Part IV: Compassion

20   While I will share some of my childhood trauma in this book, I must also acknowledge the following: I was born into a systemic culture of white privilege and wealth privilege. My parents, also a part of that systemic culture, did give me a sense in many ways that I was important; my siblings and our family were important and deeply loved. They gave us educational, creative, and athletic opportunities. My parents gave us experiences on the lake and put a pool in our backyard when I was young. That water time is, to this day, my church, my sanity, and my joy. Many of my friends came to my home. I'll never forget a junior high friend saying, when I'd apologized for my mom talking too much, "Oh I love talking to your mom. She listens and cares. My mom is never around. My maid raised me." My mom and dad were highly involved in our school-parent leadership and booster clubs. My dad was the early source of spiritual teaching for me. I have felt close with him in so many ways my entire life. Before my mom got sick, I have many memories of being with her — making handmade Christmas ornaments at the dining room table. I have fond memories of Mom putting pin curls and Dippity-DO™ in my hair before bed. My parents attended every sports game I was involved in, and to this day, if I were to call my parents and ask for a ride to the airport or to bail me out of jail, my father and mother would be there.

21   Gardner, Kay "Breathe Bigger Than Your Parts" IFS Level 1 Training, August, 2022.

22   Schwartz, Richard C, *No Bad Parts: Healing Trauma & Restoring Wholeness with The Internal Family Systems Model*, Sounds True (2021).

## Part V: Curiosity

23  View the Images at https://www.nasa.gov/webbfirstimages

## Part VII: Courage

24  Kahn, Matt, *Everything is Here to Help You: A Loving Guide to Your Soul's Revolution*. Hay House, (2018).
25  Moore, Thomas, *The Re-Enchantment of Everyday Life*, Harper Collins (1996).
26  Wridley, John. (Writer), & Wridley, John (Director). (2022). Day One [Television series episode]. In J. Wridley & C. Cuse (Producers), Five Days at Memorial; Apple INC.

## Epilogue

27  The Cleveland Clinic https://my.clevelandclinic.org/health/diseases/22233-nstemi-heart-attack

# Acknowledgements

Thank you to my teachers, mentors, and coaches — if you were wonderful I am so grateful to have learned from you. If you were shit, controlling, and afraid, I am still grateful and have learned from you.

♡ Chris Zydel, The Wildhearted Queen — for giving me a safe place to stay when I lost my shit, and for the lessons of the brush. This whole book was born out of a painting I did in the room with you and our Creative Juices Arts Sisters in Calistoga years ago.

♡ Rich Litvin, you were really the very first coach and mentor who nurtured the "BE YOU" in me. It mattered. And I'll eternally be grateful for the twenty minutes you gave me to strip and speak on your stage.

♡ Richard C. Schwartz, I don't know you yet, but decades ago you decided to be more curious with clients, you decided to compassionately listen instead of being an academic expert. You and your clients developed this way of seeing ourselves; you didn't pathologize parts, and instead you listened and learned from the inside out. As the founder of Internal Family Systems, you've spent decades getting it out in the world, and I finally found it. You didn't hoard the work, you also brought it to the layperson, to the spiritual, medical, educational, and coaching worlds. You welcome all of us to this work, and it truly has helped me meet and trust myself more than any other lens.

♡ Gabor Maté, in one weekend with you, I became profoundly clear on the most simple, logical, and human reason I chose to leave my authentic self so long ago — that need for attachment and connection. I see the world and every human in it in a whole new way. I am kinder and more compassionate to myself and others because of your work.

♡ Bill Flanigin, my husband. Our relationship teaches me so much, you teach me so much. It wasn't long ago, my body told me another reason I chose you. You are safety, you are home, you are consistency, you are the opposite of neglect. You are care — as evidenced by the talent you have for folding even the fitted sheets. Sometimes my little girl parts get scared because we are so different in so many ways, and yet, you are my home, and I love you. Thank you for writing your own books, showing me it was possible. Let's be an author couple, together, for the rest of our days.

♡ Jo Linda Crow, Mom, you have been red-line editing my work for as long as I can remember. Your edits, and knowing you and your loving and precise red pen have me, sets me free to express myself in these words from my heart. Thank you for the time and love you put into editing this manuscript. There is no one better. Thank you for always being compassionate with me, with us kids, from the very start.

♡ Heather Doyle Fraser — This book would not exist without your patience, your compassion, your skill, your professional offerings, and your exquisite content creation and organization skills. You held my vision for years, YEARS, without any scarcity or slime, only love and an almost supernatural knowing. You model compassion — you always have, and the way you hold the creative process is exactly the way I needed to be set free as a writer. Y'all, you know I'm a run on sentence freak, and typo queen and think and write in circles. Heather set the cadence to this book, she is the bass guitar, the drums, the keyboard, her notes are lovingly woven into this work, and she makes my melodies into music.

♡ Thank you Ludovico Einaudi, Fleetwood Mac, Willie Nelson, and Harry Styles for being the soundtracks that carried me through writing this book. Who knew? Writing this book would melt the parts of my being that had become cold and armored around music (because, of course, I judged myself as not "good" at music).

# ABOUT THE AUTHOR AND ARTIST

## Allison Crow

Allison Crow, M.Ed., is a life and self-leadership coach for small business owners and executives. She has been leading, teaching, speaking, writing, creating, and coaching in one form or another since the mid-1990s.

For years, she was a hard-lined performance and sales coach motivated by outside forces and an excruciating need for approval. Now, instead of being driven by hard financial goals and lifeless quotas, Allison has an unconventional and connected practice where delicious and thought-provoking conversations are centered around meeting yourself deeply. She helps her clients compassionately work with emotions, thoughts, and behaviors that are natural but often bypassed parts of our human selves. Allison specializes in IFS-informed coaching, deep inner work, creative expression, and building the skills of courageous emotional presence and self-trust.

Allison lives in the hill country outside of Austin, Texas, with her husband of fifteen years and her rescued dogs, Leroy Brown and Clementine. She is often seen with a stack of journals, a paintbrush and watercolors, with her phone in her hand, creating and connecting on social media, or floating in the backyard pool she calls her "church."

*WWW.ALLISONCROW.COM*

Made in the USA
Monee, IL
07 December 2022

20180158R00175